AGAINST THE CURRENT
Published by Hellgate Press
(An imprint of L&R Publishing, LLC)

Hellgate Press
PO Box 3531
Ashland, OR 97520
email: sales@hellgatepress.com

Interior Design: L. Redding
Cover Design: Michelle McDowell
ISBN: 978-1-954163-50-8

Printed and bound in the United States of America
First edition 10 9 8 7 6 5 4 3 2 1

*To my mother, who struggled to understand and help my father
during his times of mental suffering and stood by him
through thick and thin.*

*To my father, who lived a life rich and full,
who persisted in seeing the good in people.*

Debborah Ranniger, PhD
AGAINST The CURRENT

A Conscientious Objector During World War II
and the Daughter He Inspired

HELLGATE PRESS   ASHLAND, OREGON

AGAINST THE CURRENT

Contents

AGAINST THE CURRENT

Prologue

E ACH YEAR IN THE PACIFIC NORTHWEST, the salmon
return home in the late fall. They swim thousands of miles from
the ocean, swimming upstream through rivers and streams. Hurtling
themselves over rocks and rapids, leaping up the man-made fish
ladders to circumvent dams, wiggling through pipes under roads, or
sometimes bounding across storm–flooded roads; they return at last
to the creeks of their origin. Their purpose? To spawn and die at
home, leaving their eggs to pass along all that they have learned
through their DNA history. They leave their carcasses filled with
nutrients, to feed and nourish the next generation. Equipped with
knowledge and nutrition, the newly hatched generation will make its
way back to the ocean in the early spring, to repeat the cycle of life.

Much like the salmon, my father left his legacy, his knowledge,
and his mark on me.

This is a memoir, the story of my father, of me, of our lives
intertwined, like creeks and streams of experience braiding together
to become a great river. Influenced at a young age to live a life of
peace and work for social justice, my father served as a conscientious
objector in World War II. One of only 3,000 men in the country
working in state mental hospitals and with a few other men, helped
to spearhead and establish the National Mental Health Foundation.
As a Jewish man, he took bold risks, went against the will of his

family and community, yet made a significant and lasting impact toward raising awareness in this country about mental illness; while sometimes struggling with mental illness of his own, though never diagnosed. Much later, in the sixties, he fought hard to end redlining in the Bay Area of California and promote fair housing laws, almost losing his real estate brokerage license. Yet he persisted, and I grew up learning first-hand the importance of standing by your beliefs, fighting for social justice, and working hard for a better world, to right past wrongs, despite obstacles, setbacks, or hardships.

Paralleling my father, my strength grew from him, a small distributary branching off in new directions, from our many shared experiences and those he thrust upon me. My passions and interests flowed in their own unique course though never diverging from the overarching quest to make this a better world for all, not just some.

Chapter One

Inspiration and Awakening

I T IS QUITE POSSIBLY THE hottest night of the year and the hottest time of day, when the baking hot bricks of this apartment begin to cast their heat inward, radiating all the heat amassed during the day, yet, I have chosen this time, or perhaps this time has chosen me, to begin to try to make sense of the fragments and threads of my father's stories. Perhaps the very intense heat has rekindled the emotional heat contained within my father, his experience, and my own intense drive to share this story. How did the little creeks and streams of our lives intertwine to become one large river?

I have been aware of my father's writings and stories for quite some time. In his later years he became obsessed with recounting his time serving as a conscientious objector in World War II and the inspiration and motivation behind it, the friendship he developed at the 1929 World Boy Scouts Jamboree. He started putting together his memoir when I was in my early forties, over twenty years ago. He kept many news articles, photographs, memorabilia, a tattered banner from his boy scout days, resumes and his own hand-written accounts of his experiences from his twenties as well as letters written home, all stuffed into a large box.

Yellow: The legal writing pads my father used to write his stories

Then he started anew, re-writing, adding on, filling in and adding new stories from intervening years. Much of this work was hand-written, scratched out, written over, written above, below, in the margins and on the sides and backs of the paper. He preferred to use yellow legal pads. Then my mom intervened. She pulled out the old manual typewriter and for a time he pecked away at that. Then she bought an electric typewriter, but he wouldn't use it. So, she took over. She managed to decipher and type up a few of the stories of his experiences but finally gave up and put it all in an even larger box. In addition to all this, there were two books included in the stack: Marvin Weisbord's *Some Form of Peace*[1] and Alex Sareyan's *The Turning Point.*[2] Both books told the story of the conscientious objectors during World War II and throughout time, from different perspectives. My dad was quoted and referenced in both books. But these were not my father's whole story, nor were they my story. My father crossed out, wrote in the margins, added scads of sticky notes, exclamation points and other commentary, as though he planned to write his own version, in his voice. By the time I inherited this voluminous stack of material my father had passed, and my mother was declining. She'd long since given up trying to make sense of it all. "Here," she said, "maybe you can do something with all this."

---

1. Weisbord, M. (1968).
2. Sareyan, A. (1994).

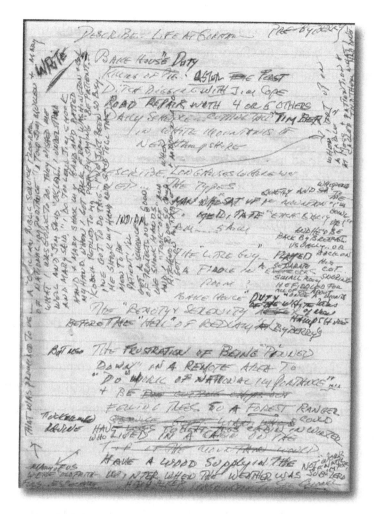

Sample of my father's writing on one of his yellow, legal writing pads

Just two months after my mother gave me this material she passed, and within the year, my husband of thirty-two years passed as well. It was 2015. I set the stack of documents in the closet and forgot about it, consumed with grief and a changed life. Until now. I had lost so much in such a short time. But this felt both timeless and timely. It was time to write. Initially, I set out to simply transcribe my father's words, to share his story, letting his voice be heard. Throughout this memoir, his voice and writings are shown in *Italics*.

As I progressed, I quickly realized that this was more. My father always noted how similar we were. My mother claimed the opposite. But where did the truth lie? Flashbacks and memories soared through my head as I read his words, my own experiences taking on new light. This was our story; a complex intertwining of our lives which shed light on my own quest for understanding and desire to make a difference.

Yellow: The color of the Star of David that Jews were required to wear in German-occupied areas during WWII.

Jews across Europe were fleeing from Hitler or just disappeared. Rumors filtering to the United States, spreading like wildfire throughout the Jewish communities spoke of atrocities being committed by the Hitler's Nazis. Those that remained were required to wear yellow Stars of David on their coats. The Jews were in danger, once again. They'd fled Egypt after centuries of enslavement, chronicled in the Old Testament, the book of Exodus. They'd fled Spain in the 1400s, Russia in the 1800s. My father's family fled from the Russian pogroms of the late 1800s, my grandfather finding kinship with the other Jewish merchants and peddlers in the 15th Ward of Syracuse, NY[3] who also had fled the violence and massacres. They began their life in the United States as pushcart merchants, selling goods off their carts in the Jewish neighborhoods. They saved what they could and worked hard to educate their children, my grandfather and other family members eventually becoming optometrists.

---

3. Onondaga Historical Association (2014).

My family tree expresses these origins, and our traditions retell the stories annually. Now, it was happening again. In 1939, Germany invaded Poland, near my father's family homeland. By the time the United States entered the war in 1941 the war had spread across Europe and Japan had attacked the United States at Pearl Harbor.

> *The bugles called the men to action, but I couldn't take the steps to join them. We had entered World War II and I received my orders from the draft board. I was determined that I would never go to war.*

One Sunday morning he announced to his family that he couldn't go to war:

> *I will not kill my fellow man and sow the seeds for another war. I will register as a conscientious objector. Shocked and dismayed, my father broke the uncomfortable silence that had descended upon the room, shouting angrily: "If you don't go to War, then I will do it for you!" "Dad, you're too old," I replied, "they'd never take you." Silence descended again.*

In the 15th Ward, everyone knew everybody. And Everybody talked, like the very gossipy ladies depicted as busybody hens through the lyrics, the actresses and the musical by Meredith Wilson, *The Music Man*:[4] "Pick a little, talk a little, pick a little, talk a little, cheep cheep cheep, talk a lot, pick a little more." Word in the family and in the community traveled fast.

---

4. Wilson, M. *The Music Man* (1962).

My Aunt Jesse said: "Len, if you dedicate yourself as an objector, you'll NEVER be able to find a job, make a living, or get married. You are committing economic suicide!" But my Aunt Roz had given a different opinion: Len, you are a leader, don't you worry. You'll get through this all right; just let me know if you need anything."

Yellow: *My grandfather called him a golden boy. Then he called him a coward.*

My father had been known as "the golden boy," bound for important things, a super achiever. His parents had sacrificed to give him opportunities. When in his teens, he had considered becoming a Rabbi. Deeply spiritual, a natural leader and desiring a life of scholarship, teaching, and helping others; he thought this was the path for him. He'd become a Scoutmaster at eighteen and director of the nearby scout camp at twenty-one. He'd been on the debate team in college, graduated from and received honors at Harvard University, the top oratorical prize; and he made the dean's list. However, after his stance on the war, the reaction of friends, relatives, and his community, he gave up on that idea and all but abandoned organized religion, or at least the practice of being part of a congregation and engaging in weekly community worship. But he never abandoned his faith or his deep-seated values and morals which grew from his religious experience. It was quite a fall from grace. But why? Why would he risk everything and make such a bold decision?

Yellow: *Like the iconic happy face, youthful and optimistic.*

It is the spring of 1929, just months before the start of the Great Depression, yet for a twelve-year-old-boy, a time of great hope and excitement.

My parents called me into the living room where my father always read the daily paper. They sat together, and my father spoke, "Your mother and I have been reading an article in the newspaper. There is going to be a World Jamboree of Scouting this summer in England. Boy scouts, 50,000 of them, will come from fifty-two countries, put up tents and cots on Arrowe Park, near Birkenhead. You will meet with scouts from all over the world, exchange souvenirs and get to know each other through many activities, parades, and events. Would you like to go?" "Yes!" I shouted, I was so excited.

Over the next few weeks my father and his parents/my grandparents made preparations, sending in the application, purchasing the special clothes needed; special knee length wool shorts and belt with loops to hold a pocketknife and a coil of rope, shirts, khaki knee socks and a special hat. The boy's shirts contained two front pockets, with the jamboree insignia sewn on the chest. Around their necks they were to wear their boy scout scarf and lanyard with whistle. They had a cool weather and a warm weather outfit.

Syracuse boys "Dressed up for World Jamboree," Left to right: Walter Blundred, Nathaniel Geddis, and Leonard Edelstein.

That summer of 1929, my father left on the S.S *Duchess of York* to Europe to participate in

Leonard Edelstein on Canadian Pacific
Steamship *Duchess of York* to England
(*Personal collection*)

the International Boy Scout Jamboree. It was early August. On the
first day of the event, he met Kiyoshi, another young scout:

> *"I am from Kyoto, Japan," Kiyoshi smiled and gave me
> his hand. I told him I was from Syracuse, in the state of
> New York. Kiyoshi had studied English and spoke it well.*

My father and Kiyoshi became fast friends. Each day they'd pal
around, touring the thousands of campsites, tromping through the rain-

soaked muddy campgrounds, meeting the other scouts, and collecting as many pins, postcards, and pictures as they could from countries around the world. Despite sleety grey skies, daily drenching, and constant mud, they set about to meet and broaden their circle of world-wide friends. Each day wasn't complete without the iconic British fish and chips.

Campgrounds, Birkenhead, England, 1929 (*Personal collection*)

> *Every afternoon there was a gigantic parade. Thousands of us marched in colorful Jamboree uniforms in front of an audience of 50,000 folks from England, Scotland, Ireland, France, Germany and more. We saluted the Prince of Wales, Duke of Connaught, Lord Baden Powell (founder of scouting), a little girl named Elizabeth[5] and other dignitaries from all over the world.*

At the end of the two weeks there was one last massive gathering where all the scouts joined together into a gigantic wheel, holding

---

5. The future Queen Elizabeth was three years old at the time of the World Jamboree.

SYRACUSE, N. Y., SUNDAY, JULY 28, 1929

Catch That Cadence!—Sergt. William H. Sheline, army sergeant, facing his troop, and his Schultz and Gerald J. Cummins, guiding their platoons, have a drill outfit of which they cuse jamboree troop, now in England. The Syracuse Scouts sailed from Montrea on July

Catch that Cadence: The Syracuse Scouts marching in Syracuse, shortly before departing for the Jamboree, 1929

hands. It was called the wheel of peace and brotherhood. At the end of the jamboree, Lord Baden Powell urged the assembled scouts to live a life of peace and goodwill.[6]

> *Then, the bugles sounded, the crowed quieted and we recited the Boy Scout Oath in unison. Tears were in our eyes. Kiyoshi and I stood together, in the mud, under a cloudy sky, then he turned to me; "Leonard, all good things come to an end, but we will write, we will stay together with our letters."*

6. ScoutWiki Network, Golden Arrow and Wheel of Peace.

When the Prince of Wales reviewed Boy Scouts from all over the world at the Jamboree at Birkenhead, England, Syracuse scouts were in the front row to salute him. The Prince is shown here with Sir Robert Baden-Powell, founder of the Boy Scouts, at the left.

Top: The Prince of Wales and Sir Robert Baden-Powell reviewing Boy Scouts, Birkenhead, England, 1929

Bottom: Boy Scout flag, ca. 1929

My father became an Eagle Scout and finished high school.[7] He went off to college to Syracuse University and then to Harvard, getting his degree in law. He and Kiyoshi continued to exchange letters up until the outbreak of World War II. Japan was now the enemy, and they could no longer write letters. They lost touch.

Yellow Peril: *A derogatory racial slur gaining popularity in the United States during the late 1800s, against Asian immigrants, particularly the Chinese, working on the railroads going to the West, and extended to the Japanese during WWII.*

It was this powerful experience of meeting and developing a deep bond with Kiyoshi, which began my father's trajectory of peace and conscientious objection when World War II broke out. When the draft notice arrived my father immediately reacted:

> *Would I stick a bayonet into the body of Kiyoshi? NO! I would rather rot in jail! At the age of twelve the pattern of the future was set in my mind and heart. I had an experience that set the mental and spiritual basis to become "a man of peace" for the rest of my life. I am a Pacifist. That was it...very simple. And my parents never talked about it again, at least not in front of me. But I knew. I had failed them. I had failed the community.*

My father took the cans of ashes from their coal stove to the street curb for Monday's pick-up. He felt good, his decision felt right. He would fill out the necessary paperwork.

Their home was small and modest, and I imagine that they could not afford steam heating, with radiators in each room, Instead, they

---

7. A boy scout who has reached the highest level of achievement in scouting.

most likely relied upon this coal stove to heat only the main part of their home, only retreating to their bedrooms at night, into beds warmed by coal warmers first.

In his speech before the draft board, he emphasized his religious objection quoting from both the Old and New Testaments. By the prophet Micah: "He has shown you, O man, what is good. Or what does the Lord seek from you but to do justly, and to love mercy, and to be ready to walk with the Lord your God?" (Micah 6:8, OSB). And the plea of Jesus: "Love thine enemy as thyself" (Matthew 5:44).

The draft board voted. He was granted conscientious objector (CO) status by a close vote, five voting yes, four voting to deny. The local newspaper reported he was being sent to prison. His father accused him of wasting his degree from Harvard Law school and pronounced that he'd ruined his life. They stopped talking to each other. This schism remained for the rest of his life.

Map of the logging camp, Gorham, NH

Chapter Two

Life in the Logging Camp

THEY SENT MY FATHER to a logging camp near Gorham, New Hampshire.

When I first saw the logging camp I thought "how beautiful," as it looked like what I remembered from Switzerland, the summer I traveled through after the jamboree. The autumn air was cool, the sun was shining, the sky clear.

Logging Camp, Gorham, NH (*Personal collection*)

To my western-raised eyes, the mountains of New Hampshire seemed more like rolling hills, rock outcroppings containing a mix of deciduous birch and evergreen trees. I grew up with towering mountains like Mt. Shasta and Mount Rainer, part of the massive mountain ranges of the Sierras and Cascades that give rise to walls of dense green redwoods, cedars, or firs, depending upon how far north you go. Still, there was a forest in New Hampshire, with sizeable trees to be cut, hence, the logging camp.

Debborah volunteering on Mt. Rainier

The camp was established at the base of a mountain. We lived in wooden longhouses, about sixty feet in length. One of these contained the eating quarters and kitchen for the whole camp. Alongside of the longhouses was a baking shed where a hundred or more loaves of bread and hundreds of cookies were baked every day.

I checked in at the camp office and carried my duffle bag to one of the large wooden longhouses and claimed an empty cot. One of my new roommates explained: "Put your duffle bag under the cot, there are no closets, and the privy is in the rear. Tomorrow we'll all be up at 7 am and we'll have fifteen minutes to be dressed and ready, then walk to the mess hall." He pointed to a building about fifty feet away. All we had to warm the longhouse was a pot-belly stove. For many months following, every day we'd cut timber and split logs.

During the Civil War, while the draft law had no provisions for those who identified as conscientious objectors, Quaker communities pressured congress to allow members of the peace churches to perform alternative service in lieu of fighting in the war. By WWI, the draft law had been amended to exempt men from military service who, "by their religious training and belief" opposed war but still prosecuted anyone else who objected and refused to enlist. Ultimately 150 objectors were jailed for life and others were harassed and beaten.

Over thirty-four million men registered for the draft with ultimately sixteen million serving in WWII.[8] Approximately 70,000 applied for conscientious objector status. Of these, 25,000 were accepted into non-combatant service, i.e., they were soldiers who agreed to work in the medical corps or any military work that did not involve combat.[9] Approximately 27,000 applicants failed to pass the physical exam, 6,000 were imprisoned for refusing to participate in any form of service. The remaining 12,000 objectors chose to engage in Work of National Importance. This was named the Civilian Public Service Program,[10] my father being one of those 12,000 men. Inspired to make a difference, just beginning to awaken to his new circumstance and the challenges that lay ahead, my father set off, full of hope.

By contrast, during the Vietnam War, more than 170,000 men were officially recognized as conscientious objectors. Thousands of other young men resisted by burning their draft cards, serving jail sentences, or leaving the country.[11]

---

8. NARA, ND. Finding Information on personal participation in WWII. National Archives and Records Administration.

9. PBS.org (2008, Oct 16). Background: *Soldiers at war WWII, Soldiers of Conscience*, American Documentary Inc.and Records Administration.

10. Nebraskastudies.org, ND. *Nebraska on the front lines – 1925-1949.*

11. The Peace Abbey(2015). Conscientious objection has a unique place in US history.

Yellowbelly: Coward, someone who would not enlist during WWII.

The people in the local community of Gorham, NH, scorned the COs when they came into town. One day, my father walked into a store in Gorham and overheard a conversation between one of the locals and the storekeeper:

> *"Yes…they got them men up in the hills cutting timber and digging ditches. Under supervision of the forest service men! They ought to be in prison!"*

My father, tall, movie-star handsome, and dressed in his plaid wool logging shirt and gear, squared his shoulders, and confidently walked up to the counter.

> *The two men stopped talking. "I'd like to purchase these candy bars please," I said, handing the storekeeper the money. "I'm one of those horrible people, the ones you think should be in prison. Do I look like a criminal?"*
> *The storekeeper took the money and spoke, "Well… no, come to think of it, you really don't. I guess I might have been mistaken about you folks."*
> *"I think you'll find us orderly and courteous, and devoutly dedicated to the idea that we human beings should not kill each other. Is that evil thinking?"*
> *There was no response from the storekeeper, then… "Uh…I think that too."*

My father took his change, replying; "Fine, I think we folks will get along well" then he walked slowly out of the store.

Double yellow line: Cross that line on the road, traffic will come from the opposite direction, right at you. Someone might be hurt.

Leonard Edelstein at the logging camp *(Personal collection)*

As a child my father would read to me at bedtime. It was usually a chapter from my favorite book, *The Wonderful Adventures of Paul Bunyan.* I'd climb into my father's lap as he sat in the brightly painted rocking chair in my bedroom. Curling myself into the space between his shoulders and knees, he would wrap his arms around me, holding the book and I'd put my ear to his chest. His deep resonant voice rumbled as he spoke. Sometimes the hairs on his chest would poke through his shirt and tickle me:

> "Paul Bunyan lived during a time when 'the forests of the Northwest were dark and immense…the trees dwarfed the men; the men had to make themselves big, if only in imagination…'"

I was certain my father was the real Paul Bunyan, especially on our first camping trip to the Feather River in Northern California when I was four years old. Each day we'd walk along the road to a little family store to buy supplies. He taught me how to cross the double yellow line safely, to walk on the wrong side of the road so I could see oncoming cars. He taught me to be safe. He seemed capable of anything, a man of action.

Red: The color of passion and romance.

My father thought when he'd made the decision to become a CO, he'd never find a woman who would dare to date him, or even go out with him. Some months before he left for Civilian Public Service, he had an opportunity to go out on a double date. My mother was attending Syracuse University, studying interior design and art, and my father lived in Syracuse. It turned out that she and my aunt, my father's younger sister, were in the same sorority. My mother was the other man's date, but my father not only had an eye for beauty and intelligence; he was an excellent dancer. He requested the pleasure of a dance with her. Out on the dance floor, sparks flew, and enough information was exchanged so that future get togethers could be arranged.

Visitors were allowed at the camp and his new love, my mother, would visit once a month. She stayed in the administrative quarters, in a room that was kept for visitors.

Yellow and Red combine to make Orange: *The brilliant colors of autumn leaves*

Of her first visit my father described:

> *I took Betty around the grounds introducing her to my peaceful brothers. My Gorham companions were really impressed as was Uncle John, one of the Quaker supervisors, along with his wife, Mary, who oversaw the pacifists. They lived in a cottage not too far from the camp. He looked at her, gave me a wink and said, "You'd better marry her in a hurry or I'm going to marry her myself."*
>
> *"Oh, come on now, Uncle John" I replied, "you're seventy-three years old, you can't marry her!" He put his thumbs in his pant straps, doubled up his fists and said, "I'd like to see you stop me!"*

My mother, winner of a baby beauty contest, lived her life glamorously. Considered by all to be photogenic and a beauty throughout her life, she wanted to be recognized for her intelligence, but often was most quickly noticed for her looks. She saw a charismatic, handsome, Harvard graduate in my father, a man with vision, bravery, and intelligence.

And so, in the logging camp on a beautiful fall day he asked my mom to marry him some day, if she'd be willing to share the hardships that he believed would befall them, including being ostracized for being a CO. Contrary to Aunt Jesse's grim prediction, she said yes.

They married in November of 1943, just over a year later. Uncle John and Mary kindly offered the use of their barn for their honeymoon, which also included living quarters. The large white brick building was

Left: Young Betty with color palette (*Personal collection*)
Right: Betty and Len Courting (*Personal collection*)

at least three stories high, with a wooden barn attached on one side and set into the hillside so that there were entrances on multiple levels. Originally it served as the residence for the farm manager and his family and a place to store their hay, grain, and animals during winter's cold. My mother made a watercolor of the building and surrounding countryside. The filtered hazy sun of autumn portends the coming winter. Only a few trees still hold onto their bronze leaves.

The marriage dinner of Betty Jane Jackson and Leonard Gerald Edelstein

Honeymoon cabin, Gorham, NH, painted by Betty Edelstein Cornell

Red, Orange, and Yellow: *Fire, the warmth of the flame.*

Winter proved grueling for my father and his cohorts. Temperatures dropped far below freezing and in only government issued Navy peacoats, wool pants, scarves wrapped around their necks and sweaters to stay warm, they'd spend each day in the weather cutting timber. Body numbing cold, mind-numbingly dull, and monotonous daily food; morale sank.

We hacked away all day. Every day we'd eat the same thing for lunch, a big pot of hot soup in an enormous jug, and either jam, baloney, or ham sandwiches. There was another jug for coffee. Once in a while we'd get a cookie. Our hands became blistered but that was no excuse for a break from the next day's cutting. Weather didn't matter either. We cut timber even when it was many degrees below zero. We'd return to the camp at days end completely exhausted. We never had fresh vegetables, mostly canned peas, or beans. Sometimes we would get canned fruit. We never got fresh fruit. Occasionally, depending on what table you sat at, one of the fellow COs would receive a cake or some candy from his family and those at his table would have a treat.

After dinner we'd go back to our long houses, heated only by the pot belly stove. Some of us wrote letters or read. One fellow had a piccolo harmonica. He'd put it to his lips and try to play a little song. He wasn't particularly good at playing it. But it was our entertainment.

Some day we are going to tell our kids, "I cut more wood than anybody else in this darn logger's camp. That's what I did." And they'll look at you and say, "Really Dad? Boy – you're like a real Paul Bunyan. Tell us some more, Dad." What is this business, we asked? Where is the work of National Importance to which we were supposedly assigned? What about projects where we could really help people?" We were told to be patient; announcements were coming soon.

My arms raised goosebumps and my spine tingled when I first discovered these passages. I recalled vividly my early memories, and our first camping trip to the Feather River, CA, flooded back in more detail. I learned how to catch trout, build, and keep a fire going by adding wood and kindling, roast marshmallows over that fire, and most importantly, to follow my own compass. My father instilled in me a strong set of values and self-worth, fortifying this with a skill set to survive and thrive. In my eyes, he embodied Paul Bunyan, larger than life itself, capable of anything and everything, a man of action, tackling insurmountable obstacles, possessing superpowers, capable of moving mountains.

NATIONAL HEADQUARTERS
SELECTIVE SERVICE SYSTEM
Washington, D. C.

.... July 27, 1942 ....

ASSIGNMENT TO WORK OF NATIONAL IMPORTANCE

To the STATE DIRECTOR of **New York**

> Registrant
> Leonard Gerald Edelstein
> 629 Clarendon Street
> Syracuse, New York

Order No. **760**   , of Local Board **No. 469, 318 Denison Bldg., Syracuse, N. Y.**
who has been classified in Class IV–E as being conscientiously opposed to both combatant and non-combatant military service is hereby assigned to work of national importance and by order of said Local Board per D. S. S. Form 50 will be delivered to:

> Camp Director
> Petersham Camp
> Petersham, Worcester County, Massachusetts
> On August 12, 1942

LOCAL BOARD PLEASE NOTE: Above registrant is to be entrained for Athol, Massachusetts. At this station he will be met by the Camp Director who will provide transportation to camp.

State Headquarters will *immediately* submit one copy of this form to the Local Board and retain one copy for its files. Note that the time for reporting to the civilian camp is specified and this D. S. S. Form 49 must reach the Local Board so that D. S. S. Form 50 can be mailed to the Registrant in time to allow 10 days' notice before reporting for transportation.

Upon receipt of this notice, the Local Board shall prepare six copies of *Order to Report for Work of National Importance* (D. S. S. Form 50). The registrant shall be sent directly to the camp specified; the Local Board shall provide the transportation and meal or lodging tickets necessary.

Lewis B. Hershey,

LEWIS B. HERSHEY,
Director.

D. S. S. Form No. 49
(Revised 6-1-42)

U. S. GOVERNMENT PRINTING OFFICE   16—20054-1

Assignment to work of National Importance, July 27, 1942

Chapter Three

Work of National Importance

T HE MORALE OF THE CAMP continued to decline. After months in the logging camp, discouraged at not doing the Work of National Importance he'd been promised, my father went AWOL.[12] He arranged with some of his fellow COs in the unit to cover for him as he wrote:

> I asked them to check me "in" on the attendance sheet and check me "out" at the end of the day so the authorities would not realize I had left. I stood by the side of the road and flagged a ride from Gorham to New York City and then to Washington DC. On a Monday morning I found my way to Col. Kosch's office and informed his secretary that I wished to see him about a very important matter.

Yellow and Blue combine to make Green: Hope, renewal, springtime.

---

12. Absent Without Leave.

Colonel Lewis F. Kosch was second in command under General Lewis B. Hershey, who directed the Selective Service System during the war. When I first read this in my father's journal, I was astonished! This was a piece of the story I'd never heard about. He went AWOL, traveling over 500 miles, at least an eight-hour trip if not more, hitch-hiking, unauthorized. And without an appointment. He just walked in, insisting on a meeting. But he did. And while this was not the first nor the last time in his life that he took bold risks and made astonishing choices; it was the first time I noticed a pattern of behavior.

My father stood his ground and waited. And waited. Until the Colonel would see him. Finally, he could speak:

> Congenially, the Colonel shook my hand. "You're a CO in the camp?"
>
> "Yes, sir, I know I'm violating the rules. I skipped out of camp without permission, but I wanted to speak to you personally. We are treated like prisoners on a chain gang. That shouldn't matter to you. We've made our decision to be COs and we can live with that decision. We are not complaining about that. But Col. Kosch, this cutting timber business is not work of National Importance. The men in Gorham and the other Civilian Public Service (CPS) units with whom we exchange letters are very frustrated. All over the country. All we want is a chance to do something of significance. We've heard that the state mental hospitals are understaffed, and underserved, what with the war effort. We'd like to help out there."
>
> He looked at me intently and said, "You have taken leave of camp without consent and hitch-hiked all the way here to tell me this?! Young man, I could have you put in jail but I'm going to send you right back to Gorham. Congress has the ultimate control. For all I know they might put you all up against a firing line. But I'll make a

*note that you want to go to a mental hospital. Where you'll
be sent, I don't know. Courage...you've demonstrated a
lot of courage in coming to see me."*

My father returned to Gorham and told his friends of his experience.
It was hard for them to believe what he had done. It was hard for me
to believe it too. And even more surprising, it worked.

Weeks later, the men's supervisor received a notice announcing
a new national program of civil and public service was finally
developed and their unit would receive details within the next few
weeks. A week after that my father received his assignment from
Colonel Kosch, to report to Philadelphia State Mental Hospital,
Byberry, within two weeks. At last, now he could be of some use.

On the bus to Byberry, riders whispered obscenities at the COs,
calling them yellow-bellies, slackers. The COs stood out because
of their youth; most men their age were away at war.

*Yellow: The color of urine, caused by the pigment urochrome, also
called urobilin.*

Three hundred mostly naked men wandered about the day room
at Byberry. A few draped themselves in pieces of burlap bags,
poorly stitched together with bits of yarn to form what looked like
a monk's habit or pants. Feces smeared the walls and ground. Urine
puddled across the floor. My father's job was to wash it away so
patients wouldn't slip or spread it further.

*The majority of the patients had only one sheet most of
the time. Many slept naked and uncovered on a mattress.
Two of us were on a shift from 10am to 7pm. We started a
mental hygiene program. We took patients to the toilet at*

Byberry Hospital Day Room 1. Photo by Charles Lord. (*Personal Collection*)

frequent intervals. My helper patients were doing this. I kept praising them, let them have leftover food and brought them candy bars.

We painted and cleaned the day room and started a feeding program to help patients to eat. I'd have to encourage many to slow down as they'd scramble for the food. 'Eat slowly; we have plenty, I'd say. I began an activities program, starting a bingo game. The next day I came in with checkers, then card games. I offered soap, cigarettes, and handkerchiefs. I put a jar in our living quarters and asked other COs to contribute.

Eddie was one of the patients at Byberry, syphilis sores everywhere; he had a gimpy leg, walking with a limp. He was a little guy, and like the others, wore shabby, filthy clothes. My father couldn't get too close as he smelled bad. He'd whistle "Dixie" constantly, breaking into a grin when someone talked to him. My father enlisted his help cleaning beds.

"Eddie, where are you?" I'd shout into the ward, a throng of men milling or lounging about on the filthy floors.

"Here I am, Boss. Here I am. How can I help you?"

"Eddie...we've got a whole ward full of incontinent patients. There must be 25-30 of them who have messed in their beds. We've got a lot to do before lunch and the nurses' inspection.

"That's ok, Boss...we'll get them done."

My father was paid only $15 a month; he used much of it for candy, chewing tobacco or other small gifts and treats for the men.

Incontinent Ward, Byberry State Hospital, 1942 (*Photo by Charles Lord, personal collection*)

We'd go to a big storage cabinet, pull out the clean sheets, blankets, and extra pillows. We would carry them to a wooden table and then begin. First, we'd strip the sleeping mats of their blankets, then, with two buckets of water and some big strips of torn up rags we'd grab and wipe off the waste. We'd take the really bad pads outside when they were really soaked and stinking. They'd stay out their till sunset or until it began to snow or rain. Eddie and I made a game out of it. I'd say "ready, set...go" and we'd both run for a pad and see who could get the most pads done in whatever time limit we set. Then we'd add up the pads to see how many pads we had done. Most of the time I'd let Eddie win. If I had done more, I'd slough off a few pads onto an empty bed frame.

My father always praised Eddie:

"Looks like you won again! How do you do it?"

And he'd break into a smile so big his whole face smiled and he'd say "Son of a gun, Boss, I don't know HOW I do it, but I DO! What's my prize for winning?"

I'd dig into my pants pocket and pretend I was having a little trouble getting to the prize...and Eddie's eyes would light up in suspense and I'd pull out slowly, a few coins, a tootsie roll or Hershey or a silly little something he could use....

I'd also say, "Eddie, we do something more, and it's better than money or prizes. We get a good feeling that we're helping them."

"A good feeling," Eddie replied. Then, he would do a little jig and say, "Oh Boss, this is wonderful, wonderful! And ya know something boss?"

I'd say, "No, Eddie what should I know?"

And he'd look at me with a big boyish grin and he'd say, "I love you, Boss!"

I'd reply, "You and I are the best bed cleaners in this whole damned hospital. I couldn't do it without you! I love you too Eddie," and I'd give him a pat on the shoulder and say, "I'll see you tomorrow, Partner, same time."

He'd do a little jig kick, like a clumsy twenty-three skiddoo, saying, "Boss, another day, another dollar, see you tomorrow!"

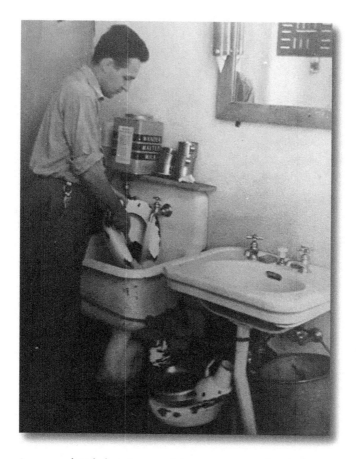

Leonard Edelstein washing out a toilet (*Photo by Charles Lord, Swarthmore Peace Collection, Harold Barton file*)

The COs introduced story hours and Victrola record concerts. The more active patients were engaged in games with medicine balls. Gradually the atmosphere changed.

The men began to respond. Two of the most fogged patients picked themselves up from the concrete floor where they spent most of their waking hours and shuffled

Byberry Hospital Day Room 2. Photo by Charles Lord. (*Swarthmore Peace Collection, Harold Barton File*)

over to the checker boards to await their turns. Both men, previously regarded as lost derelicts, suddenly began to react, to smile and talk, and to play checkers in as clear-minded a way as normal people. Other similar "miracles" began to happen. Sparks of consciousness and responsiveness in what appears to be "dead timber" have begun to appear; and they presage what might be the beginning of a return to normalcy.

Chapter Four

Action

A S A RESULT OF THEIR success and out of a desire to connect with their fellow COs working in mental hospitals across the nation, my father and his colleagues started a monthly newsletter, named "The Attendant," where they could publish and distribute observations and stories from their work and those of others (*see articles "A Job to be Done" and "Obstacles to Care and Treatment" in Appendix A*). They solicited more than 1,000 reports from other hospitals and spread information. Their goal, to improve institutional conditions, care and raise awareness. It was circulated to every federal, state and county mental institution in the country.

In one of the editions, he wrote:

> *We Americans cannot justly be proud of the way we have dealt with our nation's most important health problem. Mental Disorders affect more of us than cancer, tuberculosis and infantile paralysis combined* [and we are] *blindly indifferent to its disastrous effects, both social and economic, upon national life.*

My father decided he needed get to the top to make change. He wanted to talk to President Roosevelt, or maybe his wife, the First Lady, Mrs. Eleanor Roosevelt. Like his visit to Colonel Kosch. But how?

One of my CO brethren says he knows or has met Mrs. Roosevelt and that she is a very fine lady. But I didn't know why, or why she'd want to see me, as I was a CO and pacifist and she'd just written a scathing article about COs in her daily newspaper column titled "My Day."

She sounded as though she hated us. But my friend continued: "I've heard that one of her sons, John, wants to declare that he is a CO. The President and Mrs. Roosevelt were putting pressure on him to join the army or get into some kind of war work so they wouldn't be humiliated by his being a CO. She is very busy and travels all over the country visiting the sick and the poor and doing what she can to help all kinds of people who are in distress. I wanted her to understand that we 'objectors' were not 'slackers' or 'cowards' as she had indicated in her column and I wanted to do this directly rather than handle the situation by a letter or by phoning her, to have living proof of what we COs were doing.

My father hatched a plan. He had to be very careful. He knew that people were suspicious of the COs, that they were not trusted, not liked, in fact, despised, and any misstep could backfire. He worried that no-one would believe them. One of his fellow COs, Charles Lord, working on the wards with him, loved photography. It was his hobby. In his free time, he'd take pictures and develop them. My father decided to reach out to him.

One evening I talked to Charlie; "We are not doing work of national importance...but we can get started today or tomorrow, or whenever you are ready...we can start developing reforms that are needed and all that it takes is that little camera that you're holding in your hands! We can inform the whole nation of the conditions these poor patients live with every day! I can't do it alone, just standing and preaching and you can't do it alone either. But we can take these pictures and influence key people. People like Mrs. Roosevelt, the President's wife. And I know people who can get to them. Don't give me your answer now. It's too important to be hasty. Besides, I want to talk to some of the other men. I want to talk to Hal, Phil, and Wil. They all feel the same way I do. Wil and Phil will be cooperative. But we must not let anyone else know what we are planning until we're fully prepared. If we do let them know prematurely, we can be castigated or ridiculed by the newspapers and the authorities. Nobody must know of this until we are prepared to carry out our plan. Otherwise, our words will be considered the statements of cowards or the lies of COs who are griping about being put in institutions for the mentally ill."

The men were cooperative, but they had their doubts. After hearing my father's plan, Will Hetzel and Hal Barton, who had been on the verge of quitting, agreed to stay and help. "Leonard, it's fantastic," Hetzel remembers saying, "I don't think Selective Service will go for this. They closed down our unit in Cleveland because they didn't want us in the public eye. Go ahead and try, but you're not going to get anywhere."[13]

Yellow: *The color of gold, symbolizing success, achievement, and triumph.*

---

13. Weisbord, M. (1968 pp 37-38).

But surprisingly, the very same Colonel Lewis F. Kosch who my father had appealed to when he'd gone AWOL, hitchhiking to D.C. and back, to appeal for a transfer out of the logging camp, was delighted by the proposal. He'd seen copies of *The Attendant*, the newsletter created as part of their launch of their Mental Hygiene Program of Civilian Public Service. The aim of the publication was to describe the hospitals and develop ways to improve patients' lives and create changes nationally. Charles concealed his camera under his shirt and took pictures showing the horrific conditions. A copy had also reached First Lady Eleanor Roosevelt who sent a letter of praise, saying, "I know of your work and think it good."[14]

According to Hannah Jones in Byberry State Hospital, my father and his buddies Harold Barton, Willard Hetzel, Phillip Steel and Charles Lord had not only chronicled their own reports and photographs of the conditions at Byberry but also gathered over 1,000 reports from other federal, state and county institutions around the country reporting upon the squalid and deplorable conditions[15] (*see "Letter to Betty during Len's visit to State Mental Hospital in Staunton, Virginia" in Appendix A*).

After receipt of formal letter of request, the colonel agreed to detached service (*see "Letter to Colonel Kosch to work on Mental Hygiene program, 1944" in Appendix B*), meaning that the men could set up an office and work on data collection, reporting and expanding their program, as long as they reported to reputable medical advisors who would have veto power over their publications.[16]

The four men decided to stay at Byberry as their base to expand the Mental Hygiene Program Nationwide. According to Weisbord

---

14. Weisbord, M. (1968, p 36).

15. Jones, HK. (2013, p 72).

16. Weisbord, M. (1968, p 38).

Left to right: Phillip Steer, Leonard Edelstein, Willard Hetzel and Harold Barton (Personal collection)

in *Some Form of Peace*, my father initially led the effort with his larger-than-life vision. He was the chief fund-raiser and talking head. He was always an expansive thinker, picturing a high-budget nationwide mental-health movement with state affiliates.[17] He was passionate, visionary and was convinced raising public awareness was key (*see "Analysis of Work to be performed, detached service – Mental Hygiene Program" in Appendix A*).

In less than a year, their educational efforts were succeeding. The war had just ended, and my father and his cohorts decided to stay on after discharge to keep working on this vision to improve conditions and support for those afflicted with mental illness. They finally agreed that a non-profit model was best, with volunteers

---

17. Weisbord, M. (1968, p 41).

and public involvement and prominent sponsorships, if they were ever to effect national change.[18] My father threw his all into building support, sponsorship, and funds for such an organization.

---

18. Weisbord, M. (1968, p 41).

Chapter Five

The National Mental Health Foundation

Yellow: The color of sunrise. Golden yellow is associated with higher ideals, wisdom, understanding, and enlightenment.

MY MOTHER'S FAMILY WAS DIFFERENT in many ways from my father's. They considered themselves in the upper class of Pittsburgh and were well-enough off to have help. My mother never learned to cook because they had a cook who did all that. At the same time, they were businesspeople, as was my father's family. My mother's parents supported the family during the Great Depression with an interior design business, catering to the very wealthy, who did not suffer the impacts of the depression as greatly as others. They used their two-story brick home in Squirrel Hill, a sought-after neighborhood, as their office so it always had to be spotless and up to date for clients. They had steam radiator heating, keeping the coal in the basement and away from the furniture and fabrics. They often kept the furniture fabric covered, only revealing it for guests. Hence, they had a maid as well as the cook, to help keep everything looking lovely. They had the latest fabric coverings on their furniture, going to the expense of recovering and re-decorating every few years to stay current with changing styles. I inherited two of these beautiful pieces, a round Italian-made coffee table, the top made of Italian marble, inlaid with a chess board, encircled with branches sprouting leaves and small blooming red flowers. I also inherited my dining table, a solid heavy glass dining table for six. According to my mother both were custom designed by my grandmother. My mother attended private school and was sent off each summer to boarding camp. This was in great contrast to the much more modest wood-slat home of my father. His family, also in business, lifted themselves out of the peddler merchant class with great effort. They would likely purchase a piece of furniture to last, never replacing or recovering it. They had no hired help. Instead, my father and his sister were enlisted to do many of the daily chores, earning pennies for sweet treats. My father earned his way into scouting camp, eventually becoming a camp counselor. My mother railed against the formality of her home and family, and so I imagine that she saw in my father someone who was passionately committed to noble ideals and making a broad impact, not focusing on status, objects, things, and the impressions of others. As involved members in the Tree of Life Temple in Pittsburgh (the Temple that was bombed in 2018), her parents were horrified when they learned my mother was dating a conscientious objector, and aghast when she announced her engagement. They saw him as a renegade, a coward, and a heretic, abandoning his people in a time of great need. And, of course, they feared they'd be shamed in their community.

In September 1945, Clarence Pickett of the American Friends Service Committee (AFSC) arranged for my father and Hal Barton to visit his old friend, First Lady Mrs. Eleanor Roosevelt.[19] They brought along Lord's disturbing photos.[20]

Over tea in her New York apartment, she studied a portfolio of photographs the men had brought. One showed a crowd of stark-naked men, walking, standing in a great stone room, light from high windows reflecting off the filthy floor. In another, naked skeleton-like bodies huddled against a wall for warmth. In a third, a ragged woman, strapped to a bench, buried her face in her hands, while beneath the bench another woman hid herself from the world. Others showed the clubs, handcuffs and rubber hoses used to control patients.[21] I can only imagine just how shocked and dismayed her

National Mental Health Foundation brochure picture (*Photo by Charles Lord, Swarthmore Peace Collection*)

19. Weisbord, M. (1989 p 44).
20. Shapiro, (Dec 30, 2009).
21. Weisbord, M. (1968, p 43).

reaction must have been at the deplorable conditions of a state-run hospital, right in her own country, just over an hour's drive from her NY apartment. She agreed to sign on as one of the sponsors (*see "Letter confirming Eleanor Roosevelt's support" in Appendix C*).

My father continued his relentless pursuit. He met with civic leaders, gave speeches, raised funds, and found people to help distribute a pamphlet he wrote called: "We are Accountable" about his time at Byberry.

Pearl Buck, the famous novelist, opened the door for my father to work with public relations expert Edward Bernays and wrote a letter to him endorsing my father and the work of his colleagues. In a letter to him she wrote: "After talking with Mr. Edelstein, one of the finest young men we have met, my husband and I felt that you would be the very best person to give him advice. Please use all your heart and brains in this matter" (*see "Letter to Hal Barton reporting on meeting and letter/envelope from Pearl Buck" in Appendix C*).

Sponsors continued to sign on including Mrs. Harry Truman and retired supreme court Justice Owen J. Roberts, who agreed to become chair. They changed the name of the Mental Hygiene Program and agreed upon the National Mental Health Program, to reflect the larger vision (*see "Justice Owen J. Roberts appeal letter" in Appendix C*). Through my father's connections with the Mennonites and the Quakers, he was able to connect with editors at *Reader's Digest*, and ultimately *LIFE* magazine to publish their story. This story and shocking photographs by Albert Q Maisel, "Bedlam 1946," were printed in *LIFE* in May of 1946, the same month that Justice Roberts publicly announced the establishment of the National Mental Health Foundation.[22]

"It all started as a vision in the mind of one member of the CPS unit at the Philadelphia State Hospital, Leonard Cornell," noted Alex Sareyan, in his recounting of the events of that period in his book,

---

22. Weisbord, M. (1968, p 43).

Left to right: Phil Steer, Leonard Edelstein, Owen J. Roberts, Will Hetzel, 1945 (*Personal collection*)

The Turning Point. He was the National Mental Health Foundation's (NMHF) first executive director.[23]

Remarkably, just two months later, on July 3rd, President Harry Truman signed the National Mental Health Act, establishing the National Institute of Mental Health,[24] the first lady having been a key sponsor in the formation of NMHF.

In the first months of NMHF, education and awareness were key.

23. Sareyan, A. (1994. p 149).
24. NIMH (2017).

Several educational pamphlets were produced. My mother, now married to my father, despite her family's protests, enthusiastically threw her art school talent to the cause, designing some of the covers. On the front cover of one, titled "From Folly to Fetters to Freedom: The Story of the Mentally Ill," her initials appear at the base of the hand at the bottom of the cover (*see inset below*):

Some months later, reported Weisbord, one of his fellow founders

National Mental Health Foundation brochure cover by Betty Jane Edelstein (*Swarthmore Peace Collection*)

and CO Hal Barton, took the helm after a dispute over the direction of the Foundation. My father returned to New York (*see "Letter regarding his resignation" in Appendix C*).

Yellow ribbon: When tied around trees, fences and posts it can mean "bring our troops home."

Still shunned by his father and the local Jewish community, there was no grand homecoming, no hero's welcome for the work he had accomplished for the country on behalf of those stricken with mental illness. My first cousin, Geoffrey, well remembers the stories his mother used to tell about her brother, my father. "He was really popular, that is until he became a conscientious objector. Then a lot of people turned on him. His so-called friends turned on him. But he stuck to his beliefs. Maybe that is why he changed his name."

He and my mother legally changed their last name to an Americanized version of my grandmother's Russian maiden name. She even blotted out "Edelstein" in the signature on a quaint and rustic watercolor painting of the barn, their honeymoon accommodations, painting over it her new surname, "Cornell." It sounded less Jewish, and it disassociated my father from his father and from the Jewish community that shunned them.

Yellow: The color of gold, the great California gold rush and the golden hills of California.

He and my mother left the East Coast forever. They traveled West to begin a new life working on behalf of the community and civil rights. After a few years teaching law at the University of Denver, he became persuaded that California was a better frontier of opportunity. My parents continued West, and my father convinced my Aunt Boots, his sister, and her husband to settle in the Bay Area as well. My aunt and uncle had two children, both boys. The youngest, Geoffrey, is the same age as me, just five months apart. We grew up twenty miles apart and would get together for most holidays. They and a few cousins made their way West, but most of the family stayed on the East coast.

Over the course of my lifetime, my father only visited Syracuse once, when I was about eight, taking me with him to meet his Aunt Roz; his parents already deceased. Aunt Roz remained a solid cheer leader of my father and my family throughout his life, being something of a family mentor. On our visit, she took me shopping and bought me a charming shirtwaist travel dress, olive green with images of stamps from all over the world imprinted on it. She inspired me to pursue my dreams, to travel the world. I adored this dress and kept it long after I grew out of it.

During our visit we ate one of Schraffts's famous chocolate fudge sundaes at Blum's, the richest thickest molten fudge topping I ever tasted, sliding gently over the melting creamy vanilla ice cream. We drove by my father's neighborhood of modest wood frame houses, small, paint peeling, wood slats rotting and in need of repair here and there. The little house seemed sad and neglected, almost reflecting the strife that went on within. It was such a stark contrast to Roz's warmth and to the massive grandeur of Niagara Falls, where we explored before returning home.

While my mother and I traveled to Pittsburgh annually to visit her family, my father only came with us twice, at my mother's insistence. My grandmother had no kind words for him, my grandfather being deceased before I was born. During each visit he minimized his contact, appearing only for the larger family functions. He preferred to stay at the hotel coffee shop, enjoying the local paper, a pot of coffee and their famous pecan sticky buns or "schnecken," dripping with a caramelized sugar glaze. On occasion, he'd take me swimming at the local YMHA pool (Young Men's Hebrew Association) where he loved to swim off those buns with a half mile or so of laps.

Chapter Six

Fair Housing – Not Yet

Red Line – or Redlining: The discriminatory practice limiting credit-worthy black families from obtaining loans or living in certain parts of town.

HE WALKED THE STREETS DOORBELLING and talking to any who cared to listen. My father, now a real estate broker and civic activist, was running for city council in Palo Alto, CA. It was the fall of 1963; I had just begun the 5th grade. We were learning about how government worked. When he wasn't selling houses and running his brokerage, my father gave speeches and held campaign fundraisers. And he spent much time and energy combatting the negative publicity and gossip about his stance on fair housing, civil rights, ending redlining, and other the discriminatory practices.

Orange, blue and black: The colors my father used for his campaign logo, signs and bumper stickers.

On the campaign trail, I attended my father's rallies and events, helping stamp postcard invitations, and distributing pamphlets and donation envelopes on the chairs. I decided to do whatever I could to help campaign too. My father made promotional car bumper stickers for his campaign. They were bright orange, blue and black and I plastered the baskets of my bicycle so that every day, when I rode to and from school, everyone would see his name (*see "Cornell for Council Campaign Announcement" and "Cornell for Council Statement of Position" in Appendix D*).

"Cornell for Council" mailer

In the early 1960s, life was very segregated in Northern California. The negative publicity against my father selling homes to colored families continued as well as veiled and not-so veiled threats against my father and his business. There were phone calls, newspaper articles and individual efforts made by other realtors for him to stop.

Color – more than a pigment: *The use of the terms "colored people" or "colored families" peaked in the 1970s, when the term began to evolve, however its usage dates to as early as the 1600s.*[25]

> *It happened frequently. The phone would ring, and I'd pick up; "Len...is that you?" After cursory gestures, the caller would say, "Let's get together for a cup of coffee. We gotta talk"...or "I want to see you."*
>
> *I'd always say; "I'd love to talk." But I knew what they wanted to talk about. It was "The Problem." My fellow realtors were disturbed.*
>
> *It usually went like this: "Len, I want to help you. It's about your selling houses to minorities."*
>
> *"Oh, of course," I'd reply. You're really concerned about colored families, aren't you? You don't object to Japanese buyers, do you? After all...they're very fine gardeners." This little sentence about very fine gardeners was the statement most real estate men* [26] *would use in defending their transactions in the sale of homes to Japanese. I would stare at my host. It was like a ballet, sitting at the same table, at the same coffee shop, the same subject every time.*
>
> *"Well, yes," was the usual reply. Then the broker would say, "Len...I'm really thinking of your situation... you know...how it will affect your business...and what will it do to the Real Estate Business?"*
>
> *I would nod my head; sip a little more coffee and I would stare at him and smile. He'd look at me and appear confused, waiting for my answer. My answer was always*

---

25. Malesky, K. (2014).

26. Very few women were involved in real estate brokerage or sales at this time. Even by 1973 only 17% of realtors were women nationwide compared to 62% in 2016 (National Association of Realtors, 2016, p 9).

a question: "Tell me," I would ask, "don't you consider yourself a good citizen, a believer in our democratic system of government?"

"Of course, I do Len, I love my country and it's Bill of Rights! I am a good citizen."

"Then let me ask you one more question; I don't know your religious faith and I don't care. I have a feeling you believe in the basic precepts of most religions…such as loving one's fellow men, doing as you would be done… all that good stuff, is that right?"

"Of course, Len, of course I do."

Then I would wait. I'd sip the last bit of coffee, put the cup back on the saucer, smile in a friendly manner and say, "Thank you for the coffee! I really enjoyed talking to you, let's do this again sometime. Next time the drinks are on me."

My cousin Geoffrey has a photographic memory. Geoffrey remembers details long lost from my memory and they are astoundingly accurate and tied to key dates, places, and contain visual details. I called him to see what he might remember from our childhood and in particular, this period. He recalled that my father participated on a panel discussion hosted by the public TV station, broadcast all over the Bay Area. We were ten years old at the time and this was a really big deal, to have a family member be on TV. My neighbor across the cul-de-sac worked for the station, and though I don't know for sure, he may well have had a hand in helping to make this happen.

On the day of the event, my cousin's family gathered around the black and white Zenith TV, which was housed in his parent's bedroom, to watch a panel discussion on housing, civil rights, and the council race. When my father walked on to the stage and took his seat, they all started shouting, "Look, Leonard is on TV, there he is, there he is!"

Shortly after, the California State Real Estate Association threatened to revoke his license for his stance on non-discrimination. Weeks later, he lost the election by a small margin.

WE HOLD THESE "MYTHS" TO BE SELF-EVIDENT . . .

The California Real Estate Association has issued its own Emancipation Proclamation. By its terms the Right to Discriminate on race, creed, or color shall be perpetuated. Ten thousand dollars has been appropriated to "roll back the revolution and hold the line against freedom."

I am a member of the Association. I praise it for many past efforts. But I protest its stand on Civil Liberties. For 9 years my firm has operated on an **Open Housing** basis. We have found homes for a number of Negro families. We have done so without coercing sellers, or embarrassing buyers. The atmosphere of our negotiations has been that of sympathetic understanding to the fears and desires of both parties. Neither panic nor unfavorable publicity has resulted.

And these are the Myths we hold to be self-evident:

★ PROPERTY VALUES DO NOT DROP WHEN NEGRO FAMILIES MOVE INTO AN ALL WHITE NEIGHBORHOOD. They continue to rise.

★ GHETTOS OF NEGRO FAMILIES DO NOT ARISE MERELY BECAUSE A NEGRO FAMILY MOVES IN. Negroes are equally anxious to destroy the ghetto concept.

★ THERE IS NO NEED FOR FEAR AND PANIC. Integration is being accomplished. Negro families are displaying a real sense of responsibility to their families and neighbors. White families are responding in kind.

If we can face these Myths with Truth, we shall truly subscribe to the Declaration of Independence . . . that all men "are endowed by their Creator with certain inalienable Rights, that among these are Life, Liberty, and the Pursuit of Happiness. . . ."

LEN CORNELL,
CORNELL REALTY

Single-page flyer "We hold these Myths to be Self Evident" outlining Leonard's stance on the CSREA's practice of discrimination against Black families

Pink: The crayon originally called "flesh" that fit no one, used in a box of Crayola crayons in the 1960s. It wasn't until 1992 that Crayola began producing multi-cultural crayons including a wide diversity of flesh tones. The pink crayon was re-named "peach." [27]

Defeated, my father fell into a deep depression that lasted for what seemed like months. He left home and went up again into the mountains to his sister's cabin to gain solace. I don't recall how long he stayed but it seemed like forever. I just remember his absence. While I was only ten years old, I knew my dad had been trying to right a wrong.

Fortunately, they did not revoke my father's Real Estate License; however, by 1964, the California State Real Estate Association stepped up their campaign to "protect property values" and sponsored an initiative to counteract or mitigate the effects of the Rumford Fair Housing Act, also known as the Fair Housing and Employment Act. It was a state law banning discrimination in housing accommodations because of race, color, religion, sex, marital status, national origin, ancestry, disability, and familial status. Their new initiative to revoke the Rumford Fair Housing Act was called Proposition 14 (*see "Rumford No On Prop 14 thank you letter" in Appendix D*).

Recovered from his bout of depression, my father persisted, and threw his energy into defeating Proposition 14, chairing the Mid-peninsula Citizens Committee against Proposition 14. Unfortunately, Prop. 14 passed statewide, but was defeated in Palo Alto. Interestingly, given his loss on the city council and the statewide passing of Prop.14, my father received a Distinguished Service Award for Outstanding Community Service as a member of the Citizens' Advisory Committee on Human Relations, presented by

---

27. Crayola (2021).

The Distinguished Service Award for Outstanding Community Service received from the Palo Alto City Council and Mayor

the Palo Alto City Council and the Mayor. Additionally, the Palo Alto chapter of B'nai B'rith presented him the Brotherhood award in his efforts to preserve state fair housing laws.

The following year, 1966, the State Supreme Court overturned Proposition 14 declaring it unconstitutional. Then, in 1968, the Fair Housing Act, title VIII of the Civil Rights Act of 1968, passed, making it unlawful for any lender to discriminate in its housing-related lending activities against any person because of race, color, religion, national origin, sex, handicap or familial status.

My father was not only was charismatic, bright, imaginative and expansive in his thinking, he was a visionary.[28] His grand and often visionary ideas didn't stop. In the mid-to late 1960s he started investment groups in the Bay Area to buy land in the area around San Jose and the East Bay, the future Silicon Valley. He was extraordinarily effective in his ability to persuade others. His pitch demonstrated the trend in land values and pointed out that by being

"The Coming Land Boom in the Bay Area" by Leonard Cornell and B.L. Riback (*Personal collection*)

---

28. Sareyan, A. (1994. p178); Weisbord, M. (1968, p 41).

part of an investment group, one did not have to be rich to invest in land. Everyone could participate by owning a share. And they did.

The problem occurred when Santa Clara County, alarmed that development guidelines weren't in place to the degree that they wanted, imposed a moratorium on development in the valley. The investors panicked and all wanted out. My father was left holding the land, with demands by the investors for their money back.

I was too young at the time to completely understand the situation, but I knew we were in trouble. Suddenly everything changed. Our eating habits changed. Instead of going out to eat for dinner once a week at my parent's favorite Chinese or Mexican restaurant, we would now only occasionally do take-out from Jack in the Box or McDonald's. There were fights and arguments about money and paying the monthly mortgage. I thought we were going to lose our house. There was some question of whether my parents could help with college, just a few years away. My mother went back to school to get her MFA and then to work, teaching art and design at a local community college.

AGAINST THE CURRENT

Chapter Seven

Brokens

Violet: Red and Blue combined in various amounts make shades of purple and violet, a complicated combination of passion, emotion, grief, and depression.

MY FATHER LOVED CANDY. IT was a luxury for children during the Great Depression. He earned pennies doing chores, spending them on candy, hard candies, like Root Beer Barrels, Tootsie Rolls, and Hershey's Kisses. His favorite, the Root Beer Barrel, lasted the longest if you resisted crunching and breaking it into hundreds of tiny pieces swirling through your mouth. His love of candy and games, like the one he played with Eddie at Byberry, persisted throughout his life.

We had a tumble toy in the back yard, my favorite outdoor play toy when I was five. It was a large wooden structure, box-like, with big holes of different shapes and sizes cut out circles, squares, and triangles, at least five to six feet tall and just as wide, or wider. It was designed so you could climb into, through it, and on top of it. Why it was called the tumble toy I don't remember. I don't recall tumbling it or rolling it; maybe we tumbled through it. There were benches inside where we could sit and hide. I had four neighborhood girlfriends, all within a year of me and we loved to play on the tumble toy. My father loved to play Santa Claus. The Santa Claus game was our favorite. My dad would sing the jingle "Santa Claus is comin' to town" and then he'd disappear inside the house. We'd all scramble into the tumble toy and pretend to be sleeping. Moments later he'd emerge with little wax-paper bags of candy, the kind we used to put our sandwiches in before putting them into our lunch pails. He'd come out singing and looking for us. He'd make a great show of trying to find us and then shout, "Santa's here! Ho, Ho, Ho!!!" We'd "wake-up," peeking our heads out of one of the shaped holes and be rewarded each with a little bag of candy – most often tiny Tootsie Rolls, Hershey's Kisses or See's candies when we had them.

But by the time I was twelve, the game had changed; now things had begun to take a strange turn. At least it seemed that way to me. He'd take me to the local grocery store to shop for "brokens – bags of candy that he said other people had broken into to steal, but they'd left the bag on the shelf, opened, and still containing most of the candy. My father would find the "brokens," taking a handful of candy out of the bag. He thought it was quite the adventure. I didn't know what to do. Questions crossed my mind: *How could it be that he always found "brokens"? Was he the one breaking the bag?* It didn't feel right. I knew better.

Forty years later, I had long forgotten those grocery store trips, until one day just a few years ago.

A good friend, whose young adult son had been diagnosed with bipolar disorder, struggled to balance her work and caring for the needs of her son. There had been ongoing efforts to find the right balance of medications. He currently was not driving, and one day he called to ask if I could pick him up to help get his meds. This wasn't an unusual request. Both his parents worked. He looked up to me as kind of a mentor and friend. I had a very flexible work schedule and had helped him and his family out in this way before. In appreciation, he occasionally bestowed upon me little tokens of appreciation for helping him out: Chapstick, a small piece of candy, a pack of gum or mints.

This time it is late June in the Pacific Northwest. The damp scent of summer penetrates the air, but it's still cool enough to wear a hoodie. On the way back from picking up the meds, he says, "Let's stop at the 7-11. I want to get a soda."

We enter the store, slowly strolling down the candy aisle on the way to the drink coolers. I walk in front, then stop as he lingers to look at all the brightly wrapped candy, reminiscing about childhood favorites. Now, at the coolers, he picks up a root beer and I choose a Diet Dr. Pepper. Extra chatty today, he starts an engaging conversation with the clerk as she rings up our items. I pay for our drinks. We laugh, smile and leave, then I drive toward his house. Suddenly, he reaches down my back. Turning to him sharply, I demand, "WHAT ARE YOU DOING?" as he pulls a fistful of candy out from my hood, brandishing it about.

"Snacks," he says, smiling broadly, clearly pleased with his prowess.

I can't pull over or stop as we are on a busy arterial, and there's no parking. It's sinking in, stolen candy in my hoodie. I'd been too focused on our conversation to notice.

"That is NOT ok, you're stealing," I say. I must stay calm. Unknowingly, I just committed a crime. I am an accomplice. I'm with someone who can be volatile. Months prior on a similar errand, he suddenly jumped out of the car while I was driving around a curve, running to look for something in the bushes, beating them wildly with a stick.

He sits silently, taking this in. Despite my fear, or perhaps because of it, I keep driving.

Broken. Was he off his meds? Were they even the right meds? He's manic. And those little gifts I now realize, stolen.

My twelve-year-old self is in the grocery story, my father is finding "brokens." He's manic, just like now. More forgotten memories flood into my mind. My father is at the airport, suddenly he jumps out of our moving car to direct traffic. My mother and I scream at him to get back in the car, but we must keep moving, leaving him until we can pick him back up after our next circle around the airport. The volatile outbursts, like the Thanksgiving dinner when he became furious because my good friend and guest for dinner wanted to help mash potatoes the old-fashioned way, with a masher. He grabbed the bowl away from her, dumping them into a food processer, churning them into a gluey mess. Or the time he burst into a rage when he didn't like the way I was seasoning a Chinese dish I'd learned to cook. He stomped out of the house, sped off down the road and crashed the car. The silence and emptiness of our house when he'd retreat to his sister's cabin in the woods for days, even weeks at a time. His deep depression after the city council loss and the increasing catatonic silences where he'd just sit in his chair and stare out the window for hours.

The broken record of questions, revolving in my head for decades, even after my father's passing, halts suddenly with profound realization. My father was bipolar, just like my friend's son.

We arrive at his house. We sit in the car. My heart is still beating wildly. I am silent, as I try to calm myself and slow my brain. After a few moments I turn slowly to face him, speaking calmly and quietly, "I don't want to be a part of this. Don't do that again. And no more little gifts." He leaves the car and goes inside.

Perhaps no one knew, or the gravity of other people's stigma made it too difficult to even contemplate. This finally explained the odd behavior of my father and the question my mother and I could never answer. What's wrong with my dad? I had already begun the research for this book when this event occurred and suddenly, passages from my research took on an entirely new meaning as I read them again with a new perspective. Weisbord's quote from the other COs about his expansive and visionary thinking, his risky decision to go AWOL and meet the Colonel of the Selective Service unannounced. Everything took on a new light, new meaning. One of the passages he wrote in his journal struck me in an entirely new light.

During his time serving at Byberry, my father wrote about his observations and experiences with the different patients, Eddie being one. As I re-read these descriptions, the one about Bert now caught my attention.

> *Bert was tall, possessing a large frame, deep voice, grey hair, bold, assertive, manic – 62 years but young in appearance, a magnificent con-man type. He knows all and sees all. He has a free pass on every transport line in the country and every show and night club. He speaks as if he owns the world and sells it every 15 minutes. In reality, he is listed as an insurance broker. He speaks German, Yiddish, French, Italian and English. He speaks orations allegedly written by himself. He just wrote another song. But just now he was off on a tangent: "I was a champ bareback rider – I'd slide around on the horses belly and swing around on top of its back at a gallop, also running the finest string of horses you've ever seen, Band of Joy and Wiley Fox, lively horses I ever had, took a doctors arm off, had to shoot her, string of Australian jockeys, best in the world...." He was delusional and manic.*

Bert reminded me of my father when he wasn't depressed. He was highly intelligent, full of energy, enthusiasm, convincing others of his prowess. Others also noticed his charismatic personality and vision.[29] But sometimes he took extraordinary risks and went off track. It was the story of Bert that now really made me wonder about my father, because his description of Bert sounded like behavior I'd observed. Did my father wonder, as I suddenly did, about him – "There but for the grace of God go I?"[30] Did he see a reflection of himself in his patients? Was his abrupt departure from the National Mental Health Foundation and his role as executive director due, in part, to a wild manic swing? He swung like a pendulum across the range of emotions and behaviors, from episodes of extreme creativity, expansive, visionary inspiration and relentless activity to bouts of deep disabling depression. As time went on, the extremes became greater.

Color Palette: A wide range of colors, like emotions; the board my mother used to mix a range of colors for her art and public murals.

Back at the grocery store those many years ago, my father races ahead of me disappearing into the candy aisle. I turn into the aisle and see his hand in the bag of candy, grinning at me ear to ear. As I approach, he whispers: "Found some!" as he stuffs mini-candy bars into his pocket.

It was the shop-lifting experience combined with the bolt of realization regarding my father's behavior that compelled me to join the National Alliance on Mental Illness (NAMI). I took the signature Family to Family course, then the training to become a course facilitator.

One day, during that training we were each asked to share a

---

29. Sareyan, A. (1994, p 137).

30. Martin, G. (2017). The story that is widely circulated is that the phrase was first spoken by the English evangelical preacher and martyr, John Bradford (circa 1510–1555). He is said to have uttered the variant of the expression - "There but for the grace of God, goes John Bradford," when seeing criminals being led to the scaffold.

From Top: Mural panel by Betty Cornell of US history for Ohlone Elementary school; Mural for Palo Alto Children's Hospital; Betty at work on mural for Children's Hospital. *Left*: Betty with art palette at Ohlone Elementary School (*All from personal collection*)

story about a loved one that influenced us to become involved with NAMI. I shared the shoplifting stories about my friend's son and my father. As I ended the story, a man sitting a few seats down from me commented, "You were lucky, at least it wasn't Nordstrom!" We all burst out laughing. I had found a community that understood. I applied and was accepted to serve on the NAMI WA State board of directors.

Though I will never know for certain, it is clear to me that my father suffered from this mental illness.

Deborah at WA State Capitol, NAMI Lobby Day, February, 2018

Chapter Eight

Full Circle

Green: The grass is always greener on the other side. The color of money.

I N 1969, MY FATHER SOLD/MERGED his business with a much larger corporate real estate firm and went to work for them. They bought out the investors and took possession of the land. The local market for investors was dead.

The land acquired was choice acreage from one end of the Bay Area to the other. My father had cooperated with brokers who lived in each area. They knew the stories behind each property.

The farmer in Pleasanton has broken his spine. He wants to sell and provide a secure future for his wife and family. Two sisters in Livermore are old and wish to liquidate their assets to provide for their heirs. A Brentwood orchardist had lived out his prune trees and wanted to move to younger ones. The land was level throughout Santa Clara County and the East Bay. Each property was within two to three miles of subdivisions where growth was spilling over in the direction of our lands.

Though the local real estate market was dead, Japan had lifted its restraint against foreign investments and the Japanese loved to invest in land, often to hold for their grandchildren. My father was determined to get to Japan but had no idea where to begin.

I phoned a realtor in Los Angeles whom I'd recently met who had interests in a Hong Kong Realty firm and I explained my situation. Bill explained that he'd just returned from Japan as a coordinator for a group of Los Angeles Realtors. The trip had been under the auspices of a Japanese Company that conducted exchange tours for professionals. They had no coordinator for the San Francisco Bay area. Bill said, "Let me make a call on your behalf." From frustration and fear to the peak of excitement within an hour! This couldn't be happening.

Amazingly, within a few weeks, my father was named as the San Francisco coordinator for a real estate international business exchange, all expenses paid. While I don't recall the outcome, I expect that this is how we managed to avoid bankruptcy, by his work to engage the hearts and minds of international investors, willing to buy and hold for long periods of time.

Yellow and Red: *The sun is a yellow circle. On the Japanese national flag, it is represented as a red circle, rising sun or* Hinomaru – *"circle of the sun."*

In the spring of 1973, as part of this new role, my father was asked to coordinate of a group of realtors to visit Japan. He was part of an exchange program, and they were hosted by Japanese realtors. Business sessions were carried on in Tokyo and Kyoto. Weekends were free for sightseeing. The last leg of the journey concluded in Kyoto, Kiyoshi's home forty-four years prior. My father decided to try to find out what happened to him, if he was still alive, if he had been a Kamikaze pilot during the war, losing his life making suicidal crashes into US ships, or had he perished during the bombing of Hiroshima and Nagasaki. He approached the front desk reception to inquire on his behalf, to try to find Kiyoshi Yagi, and if they located him to say, "Leonard Edelstein – World Boy Scout Jamboree – 1929. " The woman at reception scanned the telephone book and cried out in surprise, "There are seven Kiyoshi Yagi's!" My father asked that she phone each one. She dialed the first Kiyoshi, no answer. She dialed the second, no answer. On the third, she explained her purpose, then reported: "Not your friend Kiyoshi." She tried the fourth, again. "Not friend."

But on number five she shouted, "Oh, Kiyoshi!...Your friend Kiyoshi!"

My father grabbed the phone and Kiyoshi shouted, "Leonard, where are you?"

My father told the name of the hotel and he replied, "I'm only ten minutes away – I am coming right now!"

Ten minutes seemed like an eternity to my father but suddenly, there he was, rushing through the door.

"We grabbed each other in a huge hug…like long lost brothers!"

"We stay together," Kiyoshi exclaimed! "We stay together, Leonard!

That afternoon and evening the two long-lost friends shared stories of their families and lives. My father told him what an important person he had been in his life, sharing with him how their friendship and shared experiences at the World Boy Scout Jamboree propelled him to declare his stance on peace, becoming a CO during the war. He could not go to war, put a gun in his hands and fight against the Japanese, knowing he might encounter his friend.

My father leaned closer and asked, "Tell me, Kiyoshi…did you have to go to war and fight?" Kiyoshi pulled back a little from my father and his face broke into a great big grin as he exclaimed, "No, Leonard, I was allowed to stay in leadership with the Boy Scouts and did not fight!"

He had become director of the Boy Scouts for Kyoto and now he was a member of the national board of directors.

My father shared the rest of his story about his work in mental hospitals focusing instead on how he could help his country in other ways by founding the National Mental Health Foundation, then his involvement in civil rights and fair housing; impacts their friendship carried in his life.

By the end of 1974, my father left real estate permanently and instead launched into various fundraising and advocacy ventures. I don't know what prompted this abrupt departure after over twenty years in Real Estate. It could have been that the Japan venture did not work out so well. It could also be that my father's broad and deepening emotional swings were not compatible with the high-pressure work environment of a corporate real estate company, or perhaps exacerbated by that stress.

Surprisingly, he became the key fundraiser and member of the board for the Addiction Research Foundation. Was he looking to gain insight, relief, and support for his own mental health struggles? (*Appendix F*)

The Addiction Research Foundation was established in 1974 by pharmacist Avram Goldstein, a member of our temple. He was a close friend of my father's. He was also one of the scientists who discovered endorphins, the chemicals released when you exercise.

The endorphins interact with the receptors in your brain, reducing perceptions of pain. They trigger a positive feeling, like the runner's high, similar to morphine. Goldstein was working to discover their chemical structure and better understand their role with the receptors in the brain, and how that influenced addiction and recovery.[31] Grant funds were difficult to come by for addiction research and Goldstein's dream was to raise enough funds to establish an endowment for the foundation to support on-going research in the field. My father became one of the key fundraisers to get the foundation off the ground. While Goldstein's dream fell short, during the fourteen years of the foundation's existence they were successful in contributing to significant research and publications on how the brain responds and is altered by different drugs, established the first methadone program to help recovering heroin addicts and they were able to establish an endowed chair in addiction research at Stanford University [32] (*see "Thank you letter from Senator Cranston re Addiction Research"; "Thank you letter from Avaram Goldstein Addiction Research"; "Commendation by Mayor of Palo Alto" in Appendix E*).

During this period, I became aware that my father seemed to be taking pills regularly, something I hadn't noticed before. He was also seeing a psychiatrist. There was a box at the top of his closet that I was told was off limits. One day I stood on a stool and took it down. It was filled with bottles of pills, including Darvocet, Valium, and Xanax; all of them addicting. I asked my mother what this was all about, and she just brushed it off with "Oh, your dad has trouble sleeping sometimes."

These days I never knew what might happen next, in the flash of

---

31. The Stanford Medicine News Center (2012).

32. Goldstein (1989).

a second. He became more irrational over time. On a trip to Hawaii with my mom, he started talking to people in the hotel elevator, convinced they were famous actors and greeting them as such. My mother, understandably, was mortified, not understanding what was going on nor what was happening to her husband.

Other times he'd swing wildly in the other direction. There would be days I would watch him sit in his chair for hours, facing the entry window, refusing to move because he was convinced the CIA was spying on him. Then there were other periods when he became catatonic, not speaking at all, just staring out the window. And yet, there would also be long periods of normalcy as well.

Despite his own struggles, he'd always try to help others. Both of my cousins looked up to him and would seek him out as a trusted older adult when they needed advice or counsel. Around this time Geoffrey and I were in our early college years. I had left home to go north to school, to the University of Washington, and his brother was also away at school. Geoffrey, however, still lived at home and had not yet found a direction that fit for him. My father would periodically take him out to lunch. On one outing, after lunch and a conversation about how pharmaceuticals were an up-and-coming industry, he took Geoffrey shopping, helping him to buy an interview suit, and then went about contacting various people he knew, people in the industry, to arrange introductory interviews. While Geoffrey ultimately went another direction, becoming an excellent musician, he remembered that my father always built him up and gave him confidence to pursue what was important to him.

Blue: The color of victory – a blue ribbon. The color of water.

When I was nine, my father decided it was time I learned how to give a speech. Even now I find it surprising that he would make such a declaration that a nine-year-old needed to learn public speaking and then quite emphatically follow through with it. But he did, and today I am grateful for it. He entered me into a public speaking contest at the temple, where we belonged. The speech had to be given without notes of any kind.

> *My love, I am going to share with you one of the most important tools of communication that I know. I have used it all my adult life for speeches, promotions, all types of communication, and now I am going to pass it along to you: Fresh fish for sale.*

I looked at him quizzically. "Whaaat?"

> *Eliminate the unnecessary. Even to the point of eliminating the whole statement, even the fish sign. Take out everything irrelevant. Make mental visual pictures of your key ideas. This is my gift to you.*

Instead of memorizing the speech, my father taught me how to know the basic flow of the speech with powerful phrases or images so that I could speak from my heart.

The big day came, and the congregation filled. There must have been at least one hundred, maybe more, eager parents, family members and congregants in attendance. I was the youngest speaker, which added to my terror of this moment. Then it was my turn. I slowly walked to the podium and launched into my speech. Midway through I blanked out, completely forgetting the second half of the speech. Terrified, I stared out at the audience, my heart beating wildly. Everyone was silent, waiting. Looking out from the podium, the audience and silence seemed never ending as my heartbeat grew so loud, I thought everyone could hear it. I tried looking over everyone's heads and blurring my eyes, so as not to see individual faces. That didn't work. My heart only beat faster. Then, I took a deep breath. Suddenly, all the key ideas came rushing back into my brain and I lurched ahead, finishing the speech. I was sure I'd completely failed. The audience thought differently. They roared with applause. They all thought I had paused deliberately for impact. The judges agreed. I won first prize.

Fast forward almost fifty years to 2002. I am once again about to give a speech. While I complained mightily against those early speech making lessons, what my father taught me embedded into my brain and has remained a most important and valued tool. Instead of my local temple, I am now about to give a speech to my local city council.

I am now living in the Pacific Northwest. King County had recently announced that all the swimming pools, built decades earlier by a voter supported county bond issue but now in incorporated municipalities, would be closed unless the cities accepted ownership responsibilities. The city I lived in did not want to take on the ownership responsibility of running an old pool and so the pool closed.

But not for long.

That night we filled the council chambers holding signs, wearing our caps and goggles. We were all ages, representing a broad spectrum of the community who enjoyed the local swimming pool. We had designated speakers from each swim class. I represented the lap swimmers.

I could not stand by and do nothing, being a lap swimmer and using the pool regularly. I reached out to the swim team coaches who used the pool and together we developed a plan. The coaches reached out to the families of the swim team, and I helped connect with other lap swimmers and community members. We urged everyone to come to the upcoming council meeting.

I am standing at the lectern at the city hall. My heart is in my throat, the rhythmic vibration of its beat, resounding in my chest. But this time I feel invigorated, not terrified, the surge of adrenalin powering me forward, not crippling me. My wildly curly hair is tamed into submission and submerged under my swimmers' racing cap, topped off with swim goggles gripping my forehead. I am wearing street clothes but have a towel draped around my shoulders for extra impact.

My speech covered ideas like this:

"Our pool, our community...Here before you are a cross-section of who we are in this community and this swimming pool brings us together for shared enjoyment. We come to this pool to learn to swim, to be lifeguards to save others' lives, to compete, to play. We come for health and vitality. We come to heal ourselves."

We told our stories urging the council and mayor to re-consider. Behind the scenes, we met with the city parks director and mayor and laid out a plan. A few of the folks in our grass-roots group, now over twenty people, had experience running a swimming pool. One member

Ranniger campaign re-election mailer

Left: Kent YMCA/pool opening at Morrill Meadows Park in collaboration with Kent YMCA. *Right*: New aquatic center at Morill Meadows Park. (*Both from personal collection*)

was an attorney. They proposed to form a non-profit and run the day-to-day operations if the city would take ownership of the pool. The city eventually agreed to give it a try. In 2003 the pool re-opened.

That year I ran and won a seat on the city council, serving twelve years. We used this momentum to continue to build support for the pool and over the next decade, made plans to build a new aquatic center. In 2018, in partnership with the YMCA, construction began on a new multi-use recreation and aquatic center, on land acquired by the city. The new facility, complete a modern pool designed for multiples uses opened in 2019, the doors of the old pool shuttered forever.

Though my father was still alive when I won my race for city council, due to the onset of Alzheimer's, he had lost his understanding of what being a city council member meant.[33]

My father was not alive to see me spearhead the integration of fostering diversity and inclusion into my city's strategic plan. These goals have not only remained but have continued to be reasserted, refined and broadened (*Appendix F*). He was not alive to see me testify before my state's legislative committee on the importance of funding supported housing for the long term mentally ill and chronically homeless. Nor was he alive to see me join NAMI and the governing board of the state mental hospital, to advocate for change. While I have never experienced the wild swings of mood and the behavior that accompanied them, we share the same passion for justice, equity and inclusion, and the drive to do something to improve social conditions

Before his decline, when I was in my late twenties and working on my master's degree, struggling to complete my thesis, he wrote me a letter, reminding me of his approach to communication: *Fresh fish for sale*. He also said this:

> *"I'm always intrigued by the emotional similarities that exist between us…in our feelings and reactions. When similar events occur, or [life] phases, I'm even more fascinated."*

My father always said I was just like him. My mother always said, "No, you're not like him at all, nor will you ever be." In fact, I now see that both are true.

The trajectory of our lives is forever intertwined, like little creeks and streams braiding together to become a great river.

---

33. There is a growing body of evidence that bipolar disorder increases the risk of dementia. Velosa, J. et. al (2020).

AGAINST THE CURRENT

Postscript

AFTER THEIR MOMENTOUS REUNION IN 1973, my father and Kiyoshi resumed correspondence, primarily annual Christmas cards. According to notes kept by my mother, my father stopped writing and working on his memoir in 1994. By this time, now seventy-nine years old, he had been diagnosed with Alzheimer's. In 1995, he received a Christmas card from Kiyoshi. This was the last record I found about Kiyoshi in my father's collection.

In 2018, I attended a conference on Creative Nonfiction in Pittsburgh, Pennsylvania. At the conference I struck up a conversation with another attendee and our conversation quickly turned to what brought us to the conference. It turned out that Emily was working on her PhD in Anthropology, the subject being families who lived within Tsunami areas in Japan. We both were working on research that led us to Japan, but for very different reasons. Emily kindly offered to help me research the whereabouts of Kiyoshi and/or his surviving family, as she spoke and read some Japanese. He would have been 103 at this point so I did not really expect he was still living. However, I hoped, but had not succeeded in making contact with surviving family members in hopes of gaining another perspective on the friendship between Kiyoshi and my father. Here is what Emily learned:

Kiyoshi Yagi passed away in March of 1997. At the time of his death, he was highly regarded as a leader within the Boy Scouts of

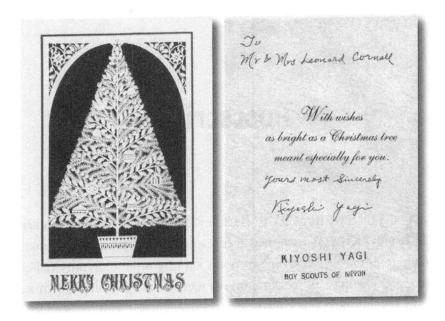

To
Mr & Mrs Leonard Cornall

With wishes
as bright as a Christmas tree
meant especially for you.
Yours most Sincerely

Kiyoshi Yagi

KIYOSHI YAGI
BOY SCOUTS OF NIPPON

MEKKY CHRISTMAS

Christmas card from Kiyoshi Yagi, 1995 (*Personal collection*)

Japan (or, rather, the Scout Association of Japan, as the organization has been known since it became co-ed in the 1970s). After the war, it seems that he did a lot to promote the Scouts, whose numbers had dropped drastically. Yagi worked directly with the American occupying forces, served on boards at the local and national level, and founded an organization in Kyoto to support the revitalization of the league there, known as the Association for the Promotion of the Kyoto Boy Scouts. As the General Secretary of the Boy Scouts of Japan, Yagi was active in organizing the 13th World Jamboree, which was held near Fujinoyima (a town at the foot of Mount Fuji) in 1971. In 1987, he was the recipient of the prestigious Golden Pheasant Award, which recognizes those who have been involved in some exceptional capacity with the Scouts. He has a son, who also made a career in the Boy Scouts.

After receiving this information from Emily, I tried, through a variety of channels to contact the son through the Boy Scouts, however, I never heard a response, and my trail went cold.

AGAINST THE CURRENT

Appendix A

Action

S U P P L E M E N T

to

Vol. I, No. 42.   "INFORMATION"   April 27, 1944

Contents: A Job to Be Done
What About Coast & Geodetic Survey?

Editors' Note: Nearly three years of experience with civilian public
service has taught us to be very exacting in our judgment of the real
work of any job we undertake. We have come to value life and time and
energy too highly to waste willingly any of these.
But here, we believe, is work of national importance. It is sent to
us as a kind of story. Anyway, it is an appeal for help from fellow
CPS men and so we're passing it on to you.

- -

A JOB TO BE DONE
By Leonard Edelstein, CPS #49

"Huddled on cold wooden benches in one large room of a certain mental hospital are
approximately 300 patients. These men arise at 5:30 a.m. and retire at 9 p.m. and
their sole occupation throughout each day with the exception of meal periods is sitting and waiting—and churning over in their sick minds the confused thoughts that
have led them to the institution.

"This is only one building of the hospital. There are many more. The patients
without occupation number at least 4000, the great majority of the patient population. This picture of one institution is typical of others in the whole country
where manpower shortage has left patients without even an essential amount of
custodial care.

"Recently there has been an influx of C.O.'s to the hospital described above, increasing the attendants' staff sufficiently so that more care can be given to the
individual needs of the patients. Introduced into the daily hum-drum existence of
these men were various games such as checkers, cards, pin-ball, ring-toss, etc. A
Bingo Nite was started with small inexpensive prizes procured by the C.O.'s given
to the game winners. Story hours and victrola concerts were conducted. The more
active patients were engaged in games with medicine balls.

"Gradually the atmosphere changed. The men began to respond. Two of the most be-
fogged patients picked themselves up from the concrete floor where they spent most
of their waking hours and shuffled over to the checker boards to await their turns.
Both of these men, previously regarded as lost derelicts, suddenly began to react—
to smile and talk—and to play checkers in as clear-minded a way as normal people.
Other similar "miracles" began to happen. Sparks of consciousness and responsiveness in what appears to be "dead timber" have begun to appear; and they presage
what might be the beginning of a return to normalcy. And the work for the C.O.
attendants, which at times has been both boring and frustrating, now proves to be
more gratifying and significant than any other work they have done in CPS.

"Here are men who are just as lonely in heart and as broken in spirit as those who
have been bombed from their homes; and here "among the missing" are derelicts who

"A Job to be Done," page 1

can be salvaged and brought back to a useful happy life in society; or failing that, they can at least be led from their deep loneliness and despair for a part of their life-time confinement.

"The task is not easy and the first couple of weeks or months of hospital work may present the new attendant with difficulties and tensions that might constitute an inner struggle for himself. But an adjustment <u>does occur</u>, and patients who origi- nally appear ugly or wretched often emerge as lovable, amusing personalities so sorely in need of a kind word or a show of attention.

"Our hospital program is progressing and we seem to be on the right road. But we need help. We need men who are willing to face the unpleasant atmosphere of a men- tal hospital ward; willing to "ride through" a period of adjustment; willing to face difficult situations and frequently long hours of work; willing to recognize in the shoddy material of human beings that will be confronted, the desparate needs for humane treatment; and willing to apply themselves to the satisfaction of those needs no matter how futile the expenditure of time and effort seems to be.

"If we can procure this help we may then be able to raise our standards of war-time treatment above the custodial level. Perhaps then we may achieve as conscientious objectors a goal in terms of human values and patterns of our society that will more than compensate for our own long hours of frustration and broken plans."

* *

WHAT ABOUT THE COAST AND GEODETIC SURVEY?
By Quentin Stodola, CPS #98

"We are perched 90 feet above the ground on the observation platform of one of our steel towers. Below us the flat plains of western Texas covered with scrubby trees stretch out to all horizons. The nearest town, and a little one at that, is over 30 miles away.

"My job is lightkeeping which simply means that I will show a light to the two ob- serving parties that are out tonight. These observing parties will accurately de- termine by means of an instrument called a theodolite the angle between my light and the lights of the other lightkeepers out tonight. The purpose of all this flashing back and forth—that is, the purpose of our triangulation survey—is sim- ply to locate some small round copper markers like the one plumbed exactly beneath the center of this tower. That small copper marker down there is certainly not a very imposing monument to our efforts. But believe it or not, and this is CPS, we think our work is important.

"We rather modestly describe our work as a permanent public improvement. Sewers, roads, oil wells, range lands, towns, farms or what have you must be located if they are to be built or used. The markers we put in are used by local surveyors as starting points to accurately survey the land so that the land may be used and improved upon.

"Besides the observing party men and the lightkeepers, we have men to build the towers and men to tear them down, men to haul the steel for the towers, automobile mechanics, men to work in our traveling office (computing and doing clerical work), and last but not least we have our cooks.

"We are really seeing the country. We stay in each town about three or four weeks, and then we're on our way again. We take long trips on back roads. We pack up to the tops of mountains and sometimes have to camp there overnight. Our next job will probably be in Nevada..."

"A Job to be Done," page 2

7

ANALYSIS OF WORK TO BE PERFORMED BY MEN ON DETACHED SERVICE
FOR MENTAL HYGIENE PROGRAM

Leonard Edelstein:

As coordinator, he would be responsible for interpreting the Mental Hygiene Program to the men in the hospitals and working with them in helping them improve the constructive service they can render the institution. His function would consist of some personal visitation, correspondence, and as coordinator for the total program, it would include The Attendant, legal survey and report, and the long-range orientation survey and the preparation of an attendant manual.

Philip Steer:

As editor of THE ATTENDANT, he would be responsible for the publication of the periodical. The editor's duties would be largely compiling and editing of material, layout work, etc.

Willard Hetzel:

As head of the legal survey and report, he would review all state laws which govern institutions caring for mental charges and prepare a legal index which will bring up to date the controlling statutes on these matters. The National Committee for Mental Hygiene is hoping that when this material is compiled, they will be able to analyze conditions of existing laws and prepare a model statute which will include the most desirable features and practices of all the states, and which could then be submitted after the war as a model law to all states.

Harold Barton:

As head of the long-range orientation survey, he would be responsible for preparing material based on experiences of the past two years which would be useful to attendants in providing better care for patients. It is hoped that this material would be available to attendants in all mental institutions and not only for CPS attendants. It is planned to prepare this in a simple, layman-like way so that it could be issued in inexpensive form and thus assure its use extensively.

Analysis of Work to be performed,
detached service – Mental Hygiene Program

THE ATTENDANT

THIS ISSUE:
The Attendant in Mental Reeducation
Statistics: Mental Disease
To the Editor

VOL. I, No. 7
DECEMBER, 1944

OBSTACLES TO CARE AND TREATMENT

By Leonard Edelstein

We present here a condensation of a paper read before the thirty-fifth annual meeting of The National Committee for Mental Hygiene, held in New York on November ninth. The original paper, uncut, will appear in a future issue of MENTAL HYGIENE.

Mr. Edelstein is program coordinator of The Mental Hygiene Program of Civilian Public Service.

●

We are far removed from the days of the witch-hunt, the "spirit-obsessed" mind, and panaceas of devils' charms and magic spells. The cries of Shakespeare's witches are mere signposts of an unenlightened age. Yet in some respects the witches might stalk today about their poison-pot and cry in rasping voices, "Double, double toil and trouble; fire burn and cauldron bubble." For this is the sorrow-song of our modern mental institutions. The obstacles which lie in the way of proper and effective care may best be characterized as "Double, double toil and trouble."

Public Indifference

Perhaps the most conspicuous problem we face is public indifference. Mental institutions are too often cloaked by the unenlightened mind in the lurid atmosphere depicted in popular magazines, and by the well-intended but deceiving veil of the institution's exterior — the short-clipped lawns, the clinging ivy on the walls of clean brick buildings. The terms "mental hospital" and "mentally ill" — intended to promote a more wholesome public attitude — too often lend false assurance that high standards are observed. Fear of criticism and political removal has prompted administrators to conceal the real problems they face — problems for the most part not confined to any particular place or person, but widespread and inherent in our whole system.

Public enthusiasm, properly focused on the defects of our system, can cut deep to the vital controls and bring forth the necessary appropriations with which wages might be boosted, facilities purchased, buildings erected, staffs increased, research encouraged, and the general standards of care and treatment thereby raised.

Developing the attitudes of those "on the outside" would seem to require the diligence and patience of sainthood and the slow evolutionary movement of any sound educational process. But what can be achieved within the institution today? What can be done now to meet the desperate cry of the war-limited superintendent who hears from all quarters, "Your needs must wait"?

Importance of Attendant

One of the most important members of an institution's staff is the attendant. In daily contact with each patient on his ward, he is a source of knowledge concerning patient behavior. Yet his knowledge is seldom tapped by busy nurses and doctors. The attendant is the one person who maintains a continuity of contact with the

(Continued on page 4)

A Publication of The Mental Hygiene Program of Civilian Public Service

The Attendant: "Obstacles to Care and Treatment," page 1

the patient, and it is these relationships that largely determine his practical effectiveness in the intricate problem of rehabilitation. By means of easeful and non-authoritarian attitudes the attendant may project, in a most natural way, a vista of desirable goals, opportunities, and promises. Above all, he should seek to counteract the stifling fatalistic outlook so inimical to mental and social upbuilding by informing himself of the encouraging proportion of mental patients who improve and get well, and acquainting the patient with the hopeful outlook by attitude rather than words — subject, of course, to the psychiatrist's advice.

The better trained attendant of the future will also know something about the role of effective reeducational methods. Primarily, he will appreciate the fact that all types of patients are capable of some degree of reeducation, that custodial care is being gradually supplanted by scientific treatment, that there has been a most significant evolution in treatment from "sorcery to science." He will appreciate the change in formal education which is gradually supplanting outworn methods of despotic control and arbitrary tyranny by systems which objectify growth, development, and opportunity for expression rather than restriction — a change that has its significant application to reeducation as well. He will understand that every sick individual is entitled to receive the treatment that will be of most benefit to him and that the difference between the regressed and the alert types, so far as reeducation is concerned, is simply the point at which the reeducative process should begin. . .

The attendant of the future will learn also the basic importance of getting the patient to do something constructive instead of dissipating and possibly distorting his available energy in evasive creation; he will impress upon the patient the "validity of the present task," the futility of "talking a good job instead of doing it" . . .

The attendant who enters upon the next decade will very probably come upon a stage where new, more social, and more compellingly humane motives will be

4

brought into play. The words of Professor Josiah Royce may help to illuminate the way for the new culture and social perspective:

"You must come now, not any longer as a disciplinarian, but quite sincerely as a friend, as a humane man offering help to a younger brother in distress... You must be a true naturalist and study this live creature as a biologist would study cell growth under a microscope, or as a pathologist would minutely examine diseased tissues. In order to study, you must, of course, love. Minds and their processes must be delightful things in your eyes... Intolerance and impatience must have absolutely no place in such a scrutiny. You must fear nothing. You will be tender with the sanctities of youthful feeling; but if, in the course of your scrutiny, a poor heart gets open to you and you find it a very evil heart indeed, you will never show — yes, if you are wise, you will seldom feel any contempt."

CARE AND TREATMENT . . .

(*Continued from page 1*)

patients, thereby enabling him to carry on in treatment what others are unable to do, yet only in rare instances is he encouraged to know the nature of a patient's illness or the treatment being administered. The attendant is the patient's major source of contact with a sane world, yet frequently that contact is made with an indifferent and even psychopathic personality, who subjugates his patients with fear, or undermines attempts at professional treatment by neglect, indifference and even brutality.

What can be done to strengthen this link with the patient — to bolster the type of care and treatment that is rendered? What can be done immediately with little or no expense to reduce the disparity between standards of care in mental institutions and those in general hospitals?

The following problems have been suggested by attendants throughout the country now united and participating in The

The Attendant: "Obstacles to Care and Treatment," page 2

My lovely Wife:

I am visiting the Mental Hopital in Staunton Virginia. This is worse than the "hell-hole at Byberry. The Attendants who work here are very old. This is probably the only job that these men can get. They look worse than the patients. If they were not working here they would probably be on the Relief Rolls. They live in dungeon cells that are similar to the ones where the patients are. They wear old clothes and they hear the gooans and shrieks of the Patients. Their salaries are forty-five dollars per month. At night they sleep in old Army cots. One Attendant said that when he first started his job he could't sleep nights. A large rat jumped on this cot and bed bugs swarmed over his body.. He couln't sleep and he was miserable.

Tonight after supper I visited the Hospital Wards. Despite the two years of conditioning by wokking here I felt sick when I realized when I walked walked through the dungeon Wards and saw the patients lying on hard floors. There were no lights....no beds to lie on. Eight to ten men would lie on bare floor. The windows were jammed tight.

I am very tired....and as usual I am frustrated and I sit here wondering "What can I do?? What can I do to help these poor sick Patients? I hear the voice of a Patient who says "Last week my Sister came. I got some word from home at last! My Sister couln't get in to see me. She couln't get in'. I could only stand at the window and wave to her. We couldn't talk to each other.... And now i wonder, "Will she ever come back ? ...Will I ever be with her again? The Hopital lights are shut off. It's the end of another day.

Good night Love....

Len

You ARE Wonder Ful!

Letter to Betty during Len's visit to State Mental Hospital in Staunton, Virginia

Appendix B

Work of National Importance

August 4, 1944

Colonel Lewis F. Kosch
Assistant Director - Camp Operations
Selective Service System
Washington, D. C.

My dear Colonel Kosch:

I would appreciate it if you would approve
the following men for detached service with
the National Service Board, to work on the
Mental Hygiene Program which we discussed
last week:

Leonard Gerald Edelstein, as coordinator of
the work and interpreter to hospital
superintendents and men.

Philip Siegel Steer, as editor of The Attendant.

Harold Edwin Logan Barton, as head of the
long-range Education Survey.

Willard Charles Hetzel, as head of the Legal
Survey and Report.

All of these men are now assigned to CPS Unit
No. 49, Philadelphia State Hospital, and we
understand that replacements would be provided
by the American Friends Service Committee for
the men.

Cordially yours,

Paul Comly French

pcf:mbr
cc/Len Edelstein
CPS No. 49

Letter to Colonel Kosch to work on
Mental Hygiene program, 1944

THE NATIONAL COMMITTEE FOR MENTAL HYGIENE
INCORPORATED
1790 BROADWAY, NEW YORK 19, N. Y.
CIRCLE 5-5000
Founded in 1909 by CLIFFORD WHITTINGHAM BEERS

ADOLF MEYER, M.D.
Honorary President

JAMES R. ANGELL, LL.D.
WILLIAM L. RUSSELL, M.D.
Vice Presidents

MRS. ALBERT D. LASKER
Secretary

HARRY PELHAM ROBBINS
Treasurer

EUGENE MEYER
President

FRANK FREMONT-SMITH, M.D.
LEONARD G. ROWNTREE, M.D.
Vice Presidents

ORLANDO B. WILLCOX
Chairman, Board of Directors

JAMES S. PLANT, M.D.
Chairman, Executive Committee

GEORGE S. STEVENSON, M.D.
Medical Director

April 9, 1945

LETTER BY [handwritten]

Mr. Leonard G. Edelstein (*counsel*)
Mental Hygiene Program of
Civilian Public Service
P.O. Box 6000
Torresdale, Philadelphia 14, Pa.

Dear Mr. Edelstein:

I have received today from Selective Service System the following letter:

"Subject: Leonard Gerald Edelstein
Philip Riegel Steer
Willard Charles Hetzel
Harold Edwin Logan Barton

"This will refer to your visit to this office yesterday when we discussed the proposed assignment of the above-named men to detached service for duty with your Committee.

"A reference to the file reveals that these four men were assigned to C.P.S. Camp No. 34, Bowie, Maryland, and were reported as having transferred on October 27, 1944. It was assumed, therefore, that these men came under your direction as of that date.

"This will further acknowledge your communications of March 5 and March 15 accepting the points set forth in Colonel Kosch's communication of February 28. It would, therefore, follow that from now on the control and reporting for these men is your responsibility.

For the Director
(signed) A. S. Imirie
Executive Officer – Camp Operations"

This, I believe, completes the authorization of Selective Service for your detachment to the National Committee. In order to avoid setting up another installation this is made a subsidiary assignment under Camp #34.

May I express my great satisfaction with this arrangement which brings together the mental hygiene interests of your group and that of the National Committee. This association is in itself an expression of appreciation for the work done by your group in the past and a confidence of its continuance into the future.

Sincerely yours

Medical Director

gss/h

Letter of Detached Service request –
the beginning of NMHF, 1945

Appendix C

National Mental Health Foundation

THE MENTAL HYGIENE PROGRAM *of Civilian Public Service*

P. O. Box 6000, TORRESDALE, PHILADELPHIA 14, PA. • Telephone: SUMerton 0521

LEONARD EDELSTEIN, *Program Coordinator*
PHIL STEER, *The Attendant*

HAROLD BARTON, *Education Chairman*
WILLARD HETZEL, *Legal Research Chairman*

October 2, 1945

Lisle Crawford
20 South 12th Street
Philadelphia, Pa.

Dear Lisle:

      In re: Mental Hygiene Program of
              Civilian Public Service

    We hope you can make use of this in your publicity.
We are certainly grateful for your cooperation.

      It is announced by the central committee of the Mental
Hygiene Program of C. P. S. that Mrs. Eleanor Roosevelt has
agreed to be a sponsor of the program as it goes forward in
its permanent stage of development. Mrs. Roosevelt has
also agreed to call together ten prominent persons to be
selected by the M. H. P. of C. P. S. to present the M. H. P.
plans to them in the hope of procuring their sponsoring
assistance. In a forty minute discussion with our new
sponsor two members of the central committee were able to
describe past activities and some of the conditions which
the men of C. P. S. have observed. Mrs. Roosevelt claimed
to have seen very distressing conditions in the past, later
commented that she was appalled by the conditions we described.

      Another interesting development has been a general
expression of assistance from Marshall Field.

      First steps for incorporation have already been taken
by the central committee, and a search is now being conducted
to determine whether the name chosen for the new organization
will be acceptable by the laws of the state for incorporation.

      Meanwhile M. H. P. central committee is preparing to
move its headquarters to a fine large brick building former-
ly a school-house, being loaned to the M. H. P. for its headquarters. This building, located near the center of Philadelphia, will place M. H. P. closer to its point of contacts,
and will provide ample space for the staff expansion that is
imminent.

Letter confirming Mrs. Eleanor Roosevelt support, page 1

2. Mental Hygiene Program of Civilian Public Service
   October 2, 1945

With the permanent organization taking real shape the central committee is strongly requesting all C. P. S. men to submit letters describing conditions which they have observed in their own experiences. Approximately 500 of these letters have been received in the past two months, and it is hoped that by demobilization over 2,000 will have been submitted. Sending of this material to the central committee is one of the most important ways in which each individual C. P. S. man can contribute to the program. From this material will be drawn the appealing story that will be directed to the American public in the form of a book, pamphlets, and other educational releases. When C. P. S. ranks are demobilized the supply of this material will be practically cut off. It is for this reason that the central committee is pleading for immediate help.

Sincerely,

Leonard Edelstein

LE:MS

Letter confirming Mrs. Eleanor Roosevelt support, page 2

WE ARE ACCOUNTABLE

This is a story of the Mental Institution. It is not a literary Symphony. It is not a glorius story that will thrill the human heart. It is an ugly story of human failure. Beyond that it is a story of human failure. It is written by one man but it is felt by many...the discouraged and the deserted. It is a plea for love and understanding and all the important elements that make for human dignity.

It is written by one man but it is felt by many...the ill treated and abused. It is written by one man but it is felt by many....the discouraged and deserted . It is the story of a mother who is crying behind the walls of a mental Hospital for a child she may never see again.; an invalid in a broken wheel chair waiting it out while a disease creeps up his spine. It is the lament of thousands of men and women who sit on one wooden benches who sit on wooden benches alone and neglected. They are Society's "missing men".

Thumb back the pages of history one hundred years and you will find these words by the author Charles Dickens. They describe a newly opened mental asylum which he he visited in America.

.......Thursday...." Everything had a lisless"Madhous Air" which was very painful...the moping idiot,cowering down with loxng,disheveled hair.... the gibbering maniac with his hideous laugh and pointed finger...the fierce wild face. There they were...in naked ugliness and horror. The Dining Room was a dull dreary place with nothing for the eyes to rest on but the empty wall, tables and chairs."

The remarkable advance in Psychiatry, Medicine and Hospital Adminis- tration had not reached the State Mental Institutions. In the basement of the Hospital where I was working there is scrawled "Dungeon Cell...

Draft of "We Are Accountable"

THE MENTAL HYGIENE PROGRAM *of Civilian Public Service*

P. O. BOX 6900, TORRESDALE, PHILADELPHIA 14, PA. • Telephone: SOMerton 0334

LEONARD EDELSTEIN, *Program Coordinator*
PHIL STEER, *Editor of The Attendant*

HAROLD BARTON, *Education Chairman*
WILLARD HETZEL, *Legal Research Chairman*

July 23

KID WE'RE ON THE WAY

I had a talk with Pearl Buck and her husband Saturday and poured out the heart to them talking about future plans on a big scale. It hit the jack-pot I think and they said they'd doo all they can to help us. They are writing to Edward Bernays, cited by Time as the nations #1 public relations man and I suggest that I tell them the same story----that he's particularly interested in the field because Sigmund Freud was his uncle.

In addition----David Hinshaw-Quaker, public relations man for Standard Oil and other big firms ahas been contacted by John Rich after I told Rich the story, and Henshaw contacted Clarence Pickett. Both of them feel our plans have real merit and a meeting is being arranged with Hinshaw and us for August.

Also---Wil and I are going to Wash. Wed. to talk to members of The American Bar Assoc. They're interested in the legal phase and there's a chance of getting wsome $ from them--as well as their backing and good wishes--re really a wonderful contact for future promotion of our legal efforts.

I'm going to try to raise 2 or 3 thousand dollares in the next 10 days. I know you'll think I'm manic---but I've got a personal bet on to see if I can do it.

Also Pearl Buck says she'll try to get us the name of prominent people who have children at Vineland for financial backing. She's caught the big view of this thing and thinks it can go.

Personal letter campaign is already paying big dividends Over 55 bathches of wonderful material in the past few weeks and promises for much more.

It's still cool here kid-but don't let that stop you from enjoying yourselves.

Sohong, now

Len

Letter to Hal Barton reporting Pearl Buck meeting

COPY FOR Mr.Edelstein

7-24 -45

July 23, 1945.

Mr. Edward L. Bernays,
9 Rockfeller Plaza
New York City.

Dear Mr. Bernays:

CORNELL

I have taken the liberty of advising Mr. Leonard ~~Edelstein~~ to come to see you, at your convenience, because I think he has ideas and plans which are extremely significant, and because he represents an unusually fine group of young men and women.

Perhaps you already know of the extraordinary work which a large group of young conscientious objectors have done in mental institutions all over the country. They have gone in as ordinary attendants, the lowest paid and most difficult jobs, and have lifted the standards of the places where they found themselves. But most important of all, they have made extremely careful ibservations and investigations in these institutions, and now for the first time we have a really reliable mass of data on the treatment of mental patients. These data mount into a shocking story, not surpassed by the sort of thing we think of as Nazi.

But it is not the purpose of these young men and women merely to accuse. In fact, they are inclined to restrain direct attacks and instead to begin a mental health educational program which will really bring about fundamental change in all treatment of the mentally ill. The American Friends Service Committee has been helping them while they collected date, but the time has now come for a very widespread campaign, both for funds and for education.

After talking with Mr. Edelstein, himself one of the finest young men we have met, my husband and I felt that you would be the very best person to give him advice. Please use all your heart and brains in this matter - indeed, I think you will when you hear all that Mr. Edelstein and his co-workers have to tell you.

Yours very sincerely,

PSW/EHM

P.S. I ought perhaps to say that Mr. ~~Edelstein~~ *CORNELL* is working on the Mental Hygiene program of Civilian Public Service, which is affiliated with the National Committee for Mental Hygiene.

*PEARL S. WALSH ?
" "PEARL" BUCK, EMINENT AUTHOR*

Letter from Pearl Buck (*Mrs. Richard J. Walsh*)

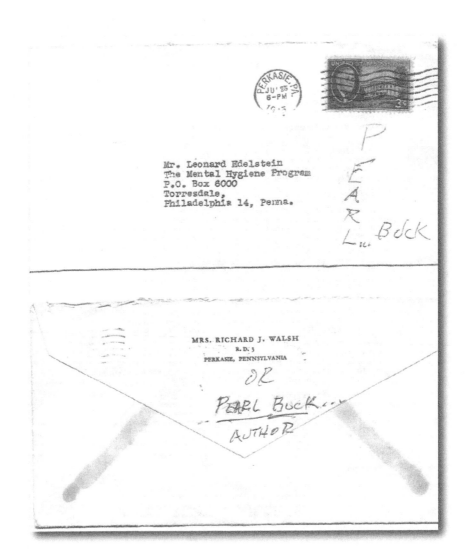

Envelope of letter from Pearl Buck (*Mrs. Richard J. Walsh*)

**THE NATIONAL
MENTAL HEALTH
FOUNDATION** ★ P. O. BOX 7574, PHILADELPHIA 1, PA.
—BARING 1548—

May 22, 1946

Dear Friend:

The National Mental Health Foundation speaks for the welfare
of 700,000 mentally ill people who are today without adequate
care in the mental hospitals of the United States. This Foundation
also speaks for the well being of an estimated eight million
people outside institutions who are suffering from varying degrees
of mental illness - some cases very slight but others most critical.

Both groups could be helped by promising new treatments. Both
groups are sadly neglected. They and society are paying an enormous
price in unnecessary human misery and in lost hours of work.

When you look at the facts as briefly portrayed by the enclosed
leaflet you will see an incredible picture. But it is true! I
have examined irrefutable evidence that in many mental hospitals,
conditions resemble the concentration camps of Europe. For a
thorough description of these conditions the article, "Bedlam, 1946,"
appearing in the May 6th issue of LIFE MAGAZINE is excellent. You
may receive complete reprints free by writing the National Mental
Health Foundation.

We must arouse vast public support so that this situation can be
remedied. Our children and our grandchildren must be protected
from an illness that today takes more hospital beds and affects more
people than tuberculosis, infantile paralysis and cancer combined.

When you realize what can be done now to wipe this scourge from
our country, I believe and earnestly hope that you will help.

Sincerely yours,

Owen J. Roberts
National Chairman

OJR:t

Make checks payable to The National Mental Health Foundation, Inc.
OFFICES AT 2580 LANCASTER AVENUE, PHILADELPHIA

Letter of support from Owen J. Roberts

Down through the Ages

society has had its class of "expendables"—the human derelicts whose names have been wiped from the list of humanity's "constructive forces." In early America they were cast out of their communities and forced to vagabond from town to town — stoned and clubbed by awe-filled townsmen. In later years they were regarded as demons, obsessed by witches' spells. Still later they were thrown into large, barren, prison-like quarters, or into the narrow confines of dungeon cells.

These "expendables" of society — these have been the mentally sick and deficient. Branded by their afflictions they have been subjected to cruel treatment by a populace that believed the old adage, "Once insane, always insane."

Recent decades of scientific achievement have brought cures and therapies for the mentally ill. Sociologists have proved that most mental defectives can lead comfortable, happy lives and be trained within the limits of their capacities. "Once insane, always insane" is as obsolete as the first automobile, yet society to a great extent still clings to false concepts of the mental patient — scorns him as the tabloid-featured maniac, or ridicules his plight in the humor of a Napoleonic caricature. And in thousands of families everywhere the mental patient is "locked in the family closet" while his past is hushed in whispers and he suffers in the loneliness of social ostracism and the neglect of public apathy.

With such real opportunities for curing the mentally ill and comforting the mentally deficient — with tremendous possibilities for preventing mental disease — we can no longer shroud our minds in false, outmoded concepts of a bygone age. With so many veterans of this war returning mentally sick, we can no longer subscribe to "Once insane, always insane." With our children facing a more complex, mind-troubling era than humanity has ever experienced, we must at last recognize insanity as an illness, and deficiency as a misfortune of birth.

NMHF brochure, page 1

$\mathcal{L}et\ us\ look$ TO THE FACTS AND FIGURES

We have given whole-hearted support to the prevention of physical diseases and the care and treatment of their victims. We have scarcely scratched the surface in the fight against mental diseases!

Mental illness strikes more persons than tuberculosis, infantile paralysis, and cancer together — yet few more than 4000 psychiatrists serve the whole nation, compared to more than 180,000 doctors for all physical illnesses;

For every ten dollars expended for physical health services, only one dollar is spent for mental health;

An estimated eight million persons are mentally ill today (one person out of seventeen);

Over one-half of all hospital beds in this country are occupied by mental patients;

Public mental institutions, handicapped by lack of funds and personnel, are often forced into low standards of treatment and care, comparable in some cases to conditions prevailing in the concentration camps of Europe. We have reports from thousands of attendants in first-hand contact with ward conditions. They have seen:

Patients beaten with clubs and rubber hoses by ill-chosen, untrained attendants;

Rushed through feeding lines like cattle;

Quartered in basement cells teeming with insects;

Choked with wet towels until unconscious;

Fed poor tasting, starch concentrated meals from grease-covered platters;

Left to sit every day, week after week, with nothing to do.

These conditions are the results of our own neglect and indifference. Just as we have settled the responsibility for concentration camp conditions upon the German people, we likewise are responsible for the horrible conditions in our own public institutions.

NMHF brochure, page 2

We can do THESE THINGS NOW

THE NATIONAL MENTAL HEALTH FOUNDATION

has been developed to help enlighten society to the true nature of mental illness and deficiency; to cooperate with others in the promotion of mental health and the prevention of mental illness; and to seek higher standards of care and treatment in mental institutions. We plan to accomplish these objectives in a number of ways. Here are a few.

TO THE PUBLIC

We will bring the story of present conditions in mental institutions;

Educational pamphlets, attractively prepared, in lay terms, to interpret the mental patient;

A program of community education for religious and civic groups to acquaint them with the needs of their own communities.

TO COLLEGES AND UNIVERSITIES

We shall appeal to students for thei: .... to encourage them to work in this field as professionals or as volunteers;

To faculties to encourage them to offer more extensive programs in mental hygiene, nursing, and psychiatry.

TO LEGISLATORS AND ADMINISTRATORS

We shall present a survey of existing state legislation to serve as a basis for further research; A set of model mental health provisions.

NMHF brochure: "Taking Action"

Sponsors

Owen J. Roberts
Dr. Harry Emerson Fosdick
Mrs. Franklin D. Roosevelt
Rufus Jones
Rep. Percy Priest
Mrs. LeFell Dickinson
Richard Walsh
Pearl Buck
Clarence Pickett
Rev. John Haynes Holmes
Arthur Morgan
Bishop W. Appleton
    Lawrence
Dr. Felix Morley
(List incomplete)

Advisors

Earl D. Bond, M.D.
Administrative Director,
Pennsylvania Hospital, Phila.
R. H. Felix, M.D.
Chief, Mental Hygiene
Division, U. S. Public Health
Service
Samuel W. Hamilton, M.D.
President-elect of The American Psychiatric Association
James Lewald, M.D.
Superintendent of the District
Training School, Laurel, Md.
George S. Stevenson, M.D.
Medical Director of The
National Committee for
Mental Hygiene
Edward A. Strecker, M.D.
Professor of Psychiatry,
University of Pennsylvania
Charles A. Zeller, M.D.
Director of the Michigan State
Department of Mental Health

Executive Committee

Leonard Edelstein, Chairman and Executive Secretary

Harold Barton, Education Director

Willard Hetzel, Legal Research Director

Phil Steer, Publications Director

Herbert Stoddard, Treasurer

Finances

Chief sources of finances to date have been the American Friends Service Committee, the Brethren Service Committee, and the Mennonite Central Committee. Budget needs for 1946 are $200,000, almost all of which will have to be raised in addition to the support of the above named agencies. All contributions will be gratefully received. Make checks payable to National Mental Health Foundation.

Headquarters
3500 Lancaster Avenue, Philadelphia 4, Pennsylvania
P. O. Box 7574 Philadelphia 1, Penna. BARing 1548

Legal Advisor
Wm. Draper Lewis, Ph.D.
Director of The American
Law Institute

NMHF brochure, back page

Office Memorandum

Date: September 4, 1946   9/5 rec.

AMERICAN FRIENDS SERVICE COMMITTEE

TO: Elmore Jackson

FROM: Donald Knoke

SUBJECT: National Mental Health Foundation

After discussing the situation at the Mental Health Foundation with several members on the Foundation staff, it appears that their internal organization is stronger than ever but that financially they are in a difficult period.

Differences of opinion about organizational structure during the past few months between Leonard Edelstein and the other staff members led to Leonard's resignation about the first of August. Leonard wanted a corporate form of organization with the staff executing policy which he and the Board of Directors would originate. This form he proceeded to implement over recurrent protests from the other staff members who maintained that the Foundation had developed on a cooperative or partnership arrangement and should continue as such.

Leonard's resignation (he had resigned several times before over similar differences) and the consequent reorganization Harold Barton as executive secretary has resulted, apparently, in a more closely knit group in feeling and purpose. From an outside viewpoint, however, the split caused some concern among sponsors of the program, prospective Board members and interested individuals. For the most part the misgivings of these individuals appear to have been resolved. Owen J. Roberts has agreed to serve as a Board member and give the program all the assistance he can. Harold Barton discussed the situation with Clarence Pickett at his home last week. Harold feels that they arrived at a mutually satisfactory understanding.

Financially the Foundation is very insecure for the moment. It is the feeling of the staff that in two months they should be on a stable basis with the income from contributions and sale of their literature and services equalling their budget. The Board will be completely selected this month and from that point the solicitation of funds should progress more rapidly. The resignation of Leonard Edelstein and the consequent reorganization also slowed the financial drive of the group.

The immediate problem of meeting payrolls, printing bills and present expenses for the next two months is relatively serious. Approximately $5,000 a month for September and October is needed to cover all such expenses--none of which is apparently forthcoming at this point. Probably the Foundation can continue operation on half this amount by postponing payment of printing bills--an arrangement agreeable to their creditors. There is the possibility they will need to cut their staff but expenses cannot be reduced by cutting salaries which are already below an adequate figure for present costs of living.

Since Clarence Pickett is already acquainted with the current situation of the Mental Health Foundation I assume that this brief report is sufficient. If you should require a more detailed account please let me know.

D. K.

Regarding the resignation of Leonard Edelstein, part 1

9/9/46

Bernard Waring   Clarence E. Pickett

This is in reply to thy note about the National Health Association. Len Edelstein was extremely able, but apparently was willing to use tactics in raising money and in publicity which a good many of the other men felt were not quite completely on the basis of integrity. That feeling grew until it was essential that the others withdraw or he withdraw. He has apparently withdrawn by request, but not with bitterness.

Harold Barton spent almost a half-day with me during my vacation to go into the whole thing. One major mistake they made was in not developing a Board to back them, to stand with them and to give advice during the early stages. Harold is now giving his full time to setting up the Board and to getting it in form. I believe the affair is going to go ahead and some of us will have to give a good deal of steadying hand to it. It is too precious an outcome of CPS not to continue.

Regarding the resignation of Leonard Edelstein, part 2

AGAINST THE CURRENT

Appendix D

Fair Housing - Not Yet

"Cornell for Council" campaign
announcement, 1963

CORNELL for COUNCIL

EDUCATION: Syracuse University, BA. Harvard Law School, L.L.B.

SPECIAL AGENT: Federal Bureau of Investigation.

ASSOCIATE PROCEDURAL CONSULTANT: War Production Board, Office of Donald Nelson. (Eliminating waste in government.)

ATTORNEY: Practice in Philadelphia, Pennsylvania.

FOUNDER & EXECUTIVE SECRETARY, The National Mental Health Foundation. (Now merged into the National Association for Mental Health.) Reform in Mental Institutions, public education, legislation.

ASSOCIATE PROFESSOR: Denver University Law School. Instructor, Temple University and Golden Gate College, San Francisco.

BUSINESS: Real Estate . . . Cornell Realty, Palo Alto.

FAMILY: Wife Betty, Artist, (Creator of "Children of the World" murals, Stanford Hospital, Children's Ward.) Daughter, Debbie, Ohlones School.

STATEMENT OF POSITION

The political drums are beating. Perhaps more than at any time in the history of Palo Alto emotions will be rising high. Confusion, personal vilification, and the clouding of issues may possibly be the result. In the desire to help prevent these evils, let me state my position.

1. I AM AN INDEPENDENT. I am not a representative of either the UNITED PALO ALTANS or the CITIZENS COMMITTEE FOR GOOD GOVERNMENT. I respect the individuals in each group as sincerely motivated in their convictions.

2. I shall conduct my campaign solely on the issues, not on personalities.

3. I shall analyze issues in terms of community welfare, not on the desires of specific interest groups.

4. I shall attempt to define terms and avoid innuendoes. Misleading banners such as "pro" or "anti-council," "residential Palo Alto" are too complex to be used without further definition.

5. In the presently confused political situation, I hope I may be a reconciling force between extreme positions; that there may be a blending of the finest values in the opposing viewpoints.

We cannot dig a moat around our City, pull up our drawbridges, and withdraw from society. We can't "Look Forward to 1940". We are living in an exciting community, and a dynamic age. But with the great advances of our time, we need not ring ourselves in walls of steel and concrete. The problems of smog, and congestion would c l o g our streets and stifle our emotions. Between the extremes is the position of a balanced community, w h e r e we allow orderly growth; where we plan to maintain balance in all facets of community life; where we do not only maintain, but increase facilities for education, recreation, and culture. T H E S E SHOULD BE THE FRUITS OF CONTINUED PROGRESS. We must be concerned w i t h planning of the Metropolitan Area. We must be concerned with the preservation of the beauty of our hills, and the protection of lowlands from floods and erosion. We should be a center of culture, reflecting the artistic and scientific talents of our community. And our gates should continue to be open to all people, regardless of wealth or ethnic and racial background.

Ours is a beautiful community. It can and will continue to be so. Stephen Vincent Benet in "John Brown's Body" aptly describes the process of growth. "My old ambition was an iron ring, loose-hooped around the trunk of a tree. If the tree grows till bark and iron touch, and then stops growing, ring and tree are matched and fulfillment fits." But if the tree keeps growing, the tree "must burst the binding ring or die." Our City will grow. We shall burst the binding ring and we shall not die. Our "fulfillment" shall fit.

CORNELL FOR COUNCIL COMMITTEE

COORDINATOR, MRS. DONALD EELS, 3888 DUNCAN PLACE, PALO ALTO, CALIFORNIA

Statement of position, "Cornell for Council" ad

Assembly
California Legislature

WILLIAM BYRON RUMFORD
MEMBER OF ASSEMBLY, SEVENTEENTH DISTRICT

CHAIRMAN
COMMITTEE ON PUBLIC HEALTH

December 31, 1964

Mr. Leonard Cornell
420 Adobe Place
Palo Alto, California

Dear Len:

We were fortunate in our campaign against Proposition
14 to have you on our side. It certainly was inspiring
to me, whenever we were being presented, to listen to
your analysis of the effects of this measure which you
presented so clearly, so sincerely, and with such logic
that your appearances were completely convincing to all
within the range of your voice. You were always able
to put forth our cause in such a manner that the average
person could not disagree.

Certainly we shall continue to work for what we think
is right, and while we lost the first round of our
battle, I do believe that in the long run justice will
prevail.

Again, thank you so much for your tremendous contribution
to what I feel was a worthy cause. We shall be looking
forward to working with you on this same project in the
very near future.

Please extend my best wishes to Mrs. Cornell and family,
and may you have a very, very Prosperous New Year.

Respectfully,

W. BYRON RUMFORD

WBR:ap

Byron Rumford "No on Prop 14" thank you letter

B'nai B'rith Brotherhood Award
Leonard Cornell

AWARD RECIPIENTS

62 WALLACE STERLING,

President, Stanford University

1963 (No Selection)

64 EDWARD M. KEATING,

Publisher, Ramparts Magazine

Area realtor receives Brotherhood Award

The annual Brotherhood Award of the Palo Alto B'nai B'rith chapter was presented to Palo Alto realtor Leonard Cornell Tuesday night in recognition of his efforts to preserve state fair housing laws.

Cornell was chairman of the Midpeninsula Citizens Committee Against Proposition 14, which waged a campaign against the anti fair housing initiative in the November election. Proposition 14, sponsored primarily by the California Real Estate Association, was approved statewide, but was defeated by voters in Palo Alto, where the citizens committee concentrated its efforts.

The Brotherhood Award was presented to Cornell by Gilbert H. Brittain, president of the Palo Alto B'nai B'rith Lodge No. 2246. More than 100 persons attended the ceremonies at Congregation Beth Am in Los Altos Hills.

In accepting the award, Cornell warned his listeners of the "real menace" of the radical right — a "dedicated minority," which he said was active on the side of Proposition 14 in the recent campaign.

Cornell said 500 rightist and racist groups spent $30 million last year on their causes, 50 per cent more than the Republican and Democratic parties combined.

Realtor Leonard Cornell wins Brotherhood Award

Palo Alto realtor Leonard Cornell will receive the annual B'Nai B'rith Brotherhood Award on Tuesday night for his efforts in 1964 to defeat Proposition 14.

The proposition, a constitutional amendment sponsored by the California Real Estate Association (CREA), was approved by the voters in the Nov. 3 election.

It nullified the Rumford Housing Act and other so-called state fair housing laws, and returned to property owners "absolute discretion" in determining to whom they may rent, sell or lease.

Cornell will be honored for successfully rallying local realtors to oppose the CREA initia-

tive amendment, and for organizing the Midpeninsula Citizens Against Proposition 14 campaign group.

The award will be presented by the Palo Alto B'nai B'rith lodge in public ceremonies set for 8:30 p.m. Tuesday at Congregation Beth Am, 26790 Arastradero Road, Los Altos Hills.

Cornell will discuss "Human Rights and the Inhuman Right" as part of his acceptance.

Last year's Brotherhood Award winner, Edward M. Keating, publisher of the Catholic lay magazine Ramparts, also will be featured on the program, according to Gilbert H. Brittain, president of the B'nai B'rith lodge.

B'nai B'rith Botherood award article

Appendix E

Brokens

A game of checkers 'neath the woods

right, under a rendering of the animal kingdom, are Judy Rock, a nurse, Ronald Hart, 8, Steven Mayo, 11, and nurse Jeanne Bryan.

n's ward shines with art

about a dozen sketches, em to her daughter, her friends, and children ospitol. Pediatrics official on several, and Mrs. nt to work. aken her about a year te six eight-by-four-foot

to do the big job was the death 2½ years ago of her son Brian, 1½. He died of a disease of the nervous system. Mrs. Cornell said she spent a lot of time in the hospital then with nothing to do, and decided her artistic talents should be put to work.

months, working from 9 a.m. to 3 p.m. in a basement research laboratory in the medical center. Her subjects included the Hopi Indians, Eskimos, Hungarian peasants, an oriental garden, and the animal kingdom. A sixth painting, showing American children of dif-

more, if a hospital art committee decides it wants more.

The material—about $300 worth —was donated by the pediatrics department and the Karen and Kristine A p p e r t Foundations. Mrs. Cornell used casein, a water based paint, sprayed with a

Palo Alto Children's Hospital news, part 1

A crib's-eye view of Eskimo land

Jeanette Miller, 7, of Stockton, enjoys a look at the frozen north, as she is wheeled by Evalyn Gart, a nurse's aide

Palo Alto Children's Hospital news, part 2

Betty Cornell US History Mural, *Palo Alto Times*

NAMI Family-to-family training completion certificate

Appendix F

Full Circle

EMBASSY OF THE
UNITED STATES OF AMERICA

Tokyo, Japan

May 15, 1973

TO WHOM IT MAY CONCERN:

Mr. Leonard Cornell, of Grubb and Ellis Real Estate, has
recently been in Tokyo and has contacted the Embassy for
assistance in establishing real estate sales to Japanese
in an effective manner. He has letters of introduction from
members of the U.S. Congress, and the Embassy has been
informed separately through the Department of State of
Mr. Cornell's trustworthiness. Any courtesies you may be
able to extend to him will be appreciated.

Sincerely,

Stephen M. Ecton
Second Secretary
American Embassy, Tokyo

Japan Embassy letter

City of Palo Alto

CALIFORNIA

OFFICE OF THE MAYOR

April 20, 1973

To Whom It May Concern:

It is my pleasure to introduce Leonard Cornell, whom I have known for more than ten years. He is a man of sincerity and integrity, and has made many valuable contributions to the City of Palo Alto. My dealings with Mr. Cornell have always shown him to be a man of highest personal integrity.

I understand Mr. Cornell is visiting Japan and Hong Kong to present opportunities in land investments in the San Francisco Bay Area, and needs guidance and assistance in meeting people who may be concerned. If you have any questions, please contact me.

Yours truly,

KIRKE W. COMSTOCK
Mayor

Mayor of Palo Alto: Letter of introduction – Japan trip

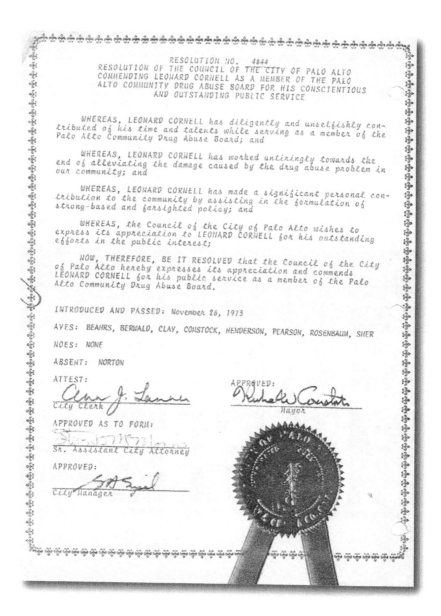

RESOLUTION NO. 4844
RESOLUTION OF THE COUNCIL OF THE CITY OF PALO ALTO
COMMENDING LEONARD CORNELL AS A MEMBER OF THE PALO
ALTO COMMUNITY DRUG ABUSE BOARD FOR HIS CONSCIENTIOUS
AND OUTSTANDING PUBLIC SERVICE

WHEREAS, LEONARD CORNELL has diligently and unselfishly contributed of his time and talents while serving as a member of the Palo Alto Community Drug Abuse Board; and

WHEREAS, LEONARD CORNELL has worked untiringly towards the end of alleviating the damage caused by the drug abuse problem in our community; and

WHEREAS, LEONARD CORNELL has made a significant personal contribution to the community by assisting in the formulation of strong-based and farsighted policy; and

WHEREAS, the Council of the City of Palo Alto wishes to express its appreciation to LEONARD CORNELL for his outstanding efforts in the public interest;

NOW, THEREFORE, BE IT RESOLVED that the Council of the City of Palo Alto hereby expresses its appreciation and commends LEONARD CORNELL for his public service as a member of the Palo Alto Community Drug Abuse Board.

INTRODUCED AND PASSED: November 26, 1973

AYES: BEAHRS, BERWALD, CLAY, COMSTOCK, HENDERSON, PEARSON, ROSENBAUM, SHER

NOES: NONE

ABSENT: NORTON

ATTEST:

City Clerk

APPROVED AS TO FORM:

Sr. Assistant City Attorney

APPROVED:

City Manager

APPROVED:

Mayor

Mayor of Palo Alto: Drug abuse board commendation

Kent Strategic Vision 2012

PROCLAMATION

Whereas, In 1890, six months after the State of Washington was founded, Kent, with a population of 793, was the second city to incorporate in King County, and was named after Kent County, England; and

Whereas, Since Kent's founding 126 years ago, we have welcomed residents from all walks of life and from all around the world, people who have built this city into the sixth largest city in the state with over 125,000 residents speaking 138 languages; and

Whereas, Kent has adopted the brand, *"Bringing the World Home,"* and promotes policies and programs to foster inclusion for all, regardless of their race, creed, color, national origin, religion, immigration status, age, mental or physical ability, sex, sexual orientation, gender expression or identity, marital status, parental status, or socio-economic status; and

Whereas, This City's prosperity as the fourth largest distribution center in the United States is built on commerce with international ties; and Kent's aerospace and manufacturing strength is led by scientists, engineers and trades people whose vision embraces not only connecting the world, but connecting people through outer space; and

Whereas, The Kent City Council adopted a vision for Kent as a safe, connected and beautiful city, culturally vibrant with richly diverse urban centers; and is dedicated to building a thriving, sustainable and inclusive community through innovative leadership, inspired teamwork and unwavering devotion to responsibly advancing our quality of life; and

Whereas, All residents, employees and visitors in Kent deserve a safe environment, free from hate, discrimination and harassment; however, if anyone feels personally threatened or unsafe, they should call 911 for immediate assistance; and anyone who witnesses someone being harassed or bullied, or a hate crime being committed, is also asked to call 911; and

Whereas, The safety of all of Kent's residents is our city's top priority; a person's right to file a police report, participate in police-community activities, or otherwise benefit from police services is not contingent upon citizenship or immigration status; and no person should be afraid to call 911 for fear their residency will be questioned, because Kent's police and public employees do not ask a person's immigration status unless they've committed a crime that results in them being arrested and booked in jail, in which case officers follow procedures from the 1969 Vienna Convention on the Law of Treaties.

NOW, THEREFORE, I, Suzette Cooke, Mayor of Kent, Washington, do hereby re-affirm

Kent is a Welcoming City

And encourage all residents, businesses, civic groups and others to express their support for our richly diverse community.

Dated this 21ˢᵗ day of February, 2017.

Suzette Cooke
Mayor

Bill Boyce
Council President

Proclamation: "Kent is a Welcoming City," 2017

EQUITY

Equity is a key value in the City of Kent Human Service Strategic Plan. We seek to:
- Promote fair and just access for community services, and building partnerships that engage in a strong commitment to equity.
- Prioritize creating an environment where diversity thrives, inclusion and belonging is the norm, and equity is the ultimate outcome.
- Invest in and work with nonprofit organizations led by and/or serving communities of color to ensure City resources reach the populations most impacted.

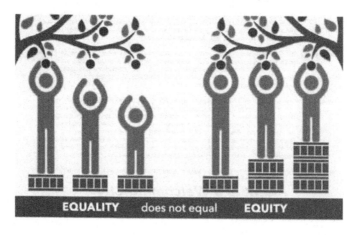

"Equity": From City of Kent Strategic Goals, 2020 – 2025

Excerpted from "The Smithsonian"
June 1978

ADDICTION RESEARCH

ADDICTION RESEARCH

Brain chemistry may influence feelings, behavior

THIS IS THE STORY THAT APPEARED IN "THE SMITHONIAN" MAGAZINE IN JUNE OF NINETEEN HUNDRED AND SEVENTY EIGHT.

Pain, pleasure, memory and even sanity could be linked to morphinelike substances produced by our own bodies

Imagine an electronic calculator landing on Ben Franklin's writing table. Within a few minutes, the inventor of the lightning rod has figured out how to use the device, but his initial delight soon gives way to perplexity. What makes the confounded thing work?

Neuroscientists today are wrestling with a similar puzzle—what makes the human brain work? They no longer describe this three-pound mass in such quaint terms as a muscle for thinking, a telephone switchboard, a piece of intellectual clockwork or an organ that secretes thought as the liver secretes bile. Even a common metaphor today—the brain as supercomputer—has proved too simplistic. Searching for a better explanation of what goes on in our heads, investigators have taken a cue from Sigmund Freud, who suspected that neuronal communication was as much chemical as electrical. In fact, Freud predicted more than 70 years ago that someday "a special chemism" would be found to explain processes underlying sexual behavior and every mental or emotional event, thus disposing of the notion that mind is independent of matter.

That day seems imminent. A whole new nervous system based on chemical substances is being mapped out in laboratories all over the world, and the new research could bring practical payoffs in treating pain, emotional disorders and drug addiction, improving intellectual performance and giving the average person a safe means of controlling his moods. And because these findings suggest the possibility of altering behavior too, they are potentially controversial.

What makes the brain different from the heart or big toe is that it processes information. Nerve cells, or neurons, communicate with each other by releasing a variety of chemical messengers called neurotransmitters. The emergence of a new class of such transmitters—called peptides—has recently proved very exciting to scientists. So much so, indeed, that some speak optimistically of a "peptide revolution."

These tiny proteins consist of amino acids strung together in a row, like freight cars in a train. Just as a locomotive may haul many different kinds of rolling stock, peptides may contain any of the 20 different amino acids that go into the key molecules of life, all assembled in a straight line.

Some peptides are hormones, and the dramatic discovery that the brain manufactures hormones to regulate its own emotions, moods and drives is taking neuroscience closer to the threshold of that special chemism which the founder of psychoanalysis envisioned. Freud's personal chemism consisted of a lifelong addiction to tobacco and a brief flirtation with cocaine. Both of these mood-altering substances are chemical cousins of morphine—that extract of the opium poppy from which the peptide awakening stems.

"What is a dire drug like morphine doing in a nice place like the brain of Man?" So mused Stanford University psychopharmacologist Avram Goldstein in 1971. In studying why narcotics cause addiction, he and his research team, working with mice, set the stage for the later discovery of natural opiate receptors in the human brain. It is startling to think that certain cells in the brains of Man and other mammals evolved for millions of years in order to embrace an extract of *Papaver somniferum*, the "sleep-bearing" opium poppy! A likelier explanation: these cells are fooled by morphine, whose structure is close to that of substances manufactured by the brain itself.

In the early 1970s, some researchers began hunting for that supposed substance—the brain's own morphine—secreted as an internal pain-killer and mood lifter. If they could isolate or synthesize this secretion it might have medical significance, for even in large doses it might not be addictive—being a product of the body itself, not an alien seed. The substance was first isolated at the University of Aberdeen, Scotland, in December 1975 by neuroscientists John Hughes and Hans W. Kosterlitz, who extracted a small opiatelike peptide from pig brains. They christened this chemical enkephalin, meaning "in the head." Compared to morphine, enkephalin proved to be a simple little molecule, a five-amino-acid chain.

David N. Leff, a senior writer with Medical World News, reports on biomedical research—from molecules and mice to Man himself.

Smithsonian Excerpt:
"Brain Chemistry may influence feelings, behavior"

References

Aufderheide, D.H. April 1, 2014. "Mental Illness in America's Jails and Prisons: Toward A Public Safety/Public Health Model." *Health Affairs Blog,* Project Hope. http://healthaffairs.org/blog/2014/04/01/mental-illness-in-americas-jails-and-prisons-toward-a-public-safetypublic-health-model/.

Auferheide, D.H. and Brown, P.H. February, 2005. "Crisis in Corrections: The Mentally Ill in America's Prison." *Corrections Today.* Vol. 67, Issue 1, 30-33. http://healthaffairs.org/blog/2014/04/01/mental-illness-in-americas-jails-and-prisons-toward-a-public-safetypublic-health-model/.

Black, A. 1966. *Casting Her Own Shadow: Eleanor Roosevelt and the Shaping of Postwar Liberalism.* New York: Columbia University Press.https://erpapers.columbian.gwu.edu/my-day The Eleanor Roosevelt Papers July 23, 2017.

Na (2021) Crayola. https://www.crayola.com/faq/another-topic/when-did-you-introduce-crayola-multicultural-products/.

Denser, L. 2020. *History of the Japanese Flag.* https://voyapon.com/japanese-flag-history/.

Dontstigmame June 7, 2017. Psychiatric Bed Crisis. *Don't Stigmatize Me.* Blog at worldpress.co. https://dontstigmame.com/2017/06/07/psychiatric-bed-crisis/.

Ganzel, B. Aug 19. 2021. Farming in the 1940s-Conscientious Objectors. Wessels Living History Farm: https://livinghistoryfarm.org/farmingthe40s/life_05.html.

Jones, H.K. 2013. B*yberry State Hospital.* Charleston, SC: Arcadia Publishing: 66.

Kerby, S. Mar 13, 2012. *Race and Ethnicity.* Center for American Progress.

Lisak, B. About colors: All about colors in one place. https://www.about-colors.com/gold-color-meaning/.

Malesky, K. 2014. "Code Switch; Race in your Face: The journey from 'colored' to 'minorities' to 'people of color.'" https://www.npr.org/sections/code-switch/2014/03/30/295931070//the-journey-from-colored-to-minorities-to-people-of-color.

Mennonite Central Committee. 2015. The Civilian Public Service story; living peace at a time of war. http://civilianpublicservice.org/.

NARA. Finding Information on personal participation in WWII. National Archives and Records Administration. https://www.archives.gov/files/research/military/ww2/ww2-participation.pdf.

National Association of Realtors. 2017. Field guide to women in Real Estate. https://www.nar.realtor/field-guides/field-guide-to-women-in-real-estate.

National Association of Realtors. 2016. Member Profile. http://www.realtorstripleplay.com/wp-content/uploads/2016/06/2016-member-profile-05-19-2016.pdf, p 9.

Nebraskastudies.org. Nebraska on the front lines – 1925-1949. http://www.nebraskastudies.org/0800/frameset_reset.html?http://www.nebraskastudies.org/0800/stories/0801_0107.html.

NIMH. 2017. Important events in NIMH history. NIH Turning Discovery into Health. https://www.nih.gov/about-nih/what-we-do/nih-almanac/national-institute-mental-health-nimh#events.

Norton, W. 2013. *Cultural Geography: Environments, Landscapes, Identities, Inequalities.* Oxford, UK: Oxford University Press.

Onondaga Historical Association. 2014. *The History of Syracuse's Jewish Community.* https://www.cnyhistory.org/2014/12/jewish-community/ August 28, 2021.

Pan, D. 2013. "TIMELINE: Deinstitutionalization and Its Consequences: How deinstitutionalization moved thousands of mentally ill people out of hospitals—and into jails and prisons." http://www.motherjones.com/politics/2013/04/timeline-mental-health-america/.

PBS.org. Oct 16, 2008. "Background: Soldiers at war WWII, Soldiers of conscience." American Documentary Inc. http://www.pbs.org/pov/soldiersofconscience/background/.

Sareyan, A. 1994. *The Turning Point,* Washington, D.C.: American Psychiatric Press: 137, 149, 178.

ScoutWiki Network. https://en.scoutwiki.org/Golden_Arrow_(Scouting)

Seto, B.F. 2015. *Paternalism and Peril: Shifting U.S. Racial Perceptions of the Japanese and Chinese Peoples from World War II to the Early Cold War.* Canberra, Australia: Asia Pacific Press.

Smith, K. 2005-2019. Color symbolism and meaning of color green. https:///www. sensationalcolor.com/meaning-of-green/.

Shapiro, J. Dec 30, 2009. WWII Pacifists exposed mental ward horrors. "All Things Considered." http://www.npr.org/templates/story/story.php?storyId=122017757.

The Eleanor Roosevelt Papers Project. 2006-2017. https://www2.gwu.edu/~erpapers/myday/aboutmyday.cfm.

The Peace Abbey. 2015. Conscientious objection has a unique place in US history. https://www.peaceabbey.org/programs-projects/conscientious-objectors/ August 30, 2021.

Untermeyer, L. 1945. *The Wonderful Adventures of Paul Bunyan.* NewYork, NY: The Heritage Press.

U.S. Scouting Service Project. 1994-2017. Boy Scout Oath, Law, Motto and Slogan and the Outdoor Code. http://usscouts.org/advance/boyscoutsoathlaw.asp.

Velosa, J., Delgado, A., Finger, E., Berk, M., Kapczinski, F. & Cardoso, T. D. A. 2020. Risk of dementia in bipolar disorder and the interplay of lithium: a systematic review and meta-analyses. *ACTA PSYCHIATRICA SCANDINAVICA*, 141 (6), pp.510-521.https://onlinelibrary.wiley.com/doi/10.1111/acps.13153

Weisbord, M.R. 1968. *Some Form of Peace.* New York: Viking Press. pp 36-38, 41-44

Acknowledgments

WITHOUT THE HELP AND ENCOURAGEMENT of many people, this book would not have been possible. The material passed on to me by my mother only told part of the story. I thank the following people who helped me fill in the missing pieces: Wendy E. Chmielewski and the Swarthmore Peace Collection librarians for helping me access documents that helped fill in the missing pieces; Maria Santelli, Executive Director of Center on Conscience & War, who gave me permission to access critical documents regarding the work of conscientious objectors during WWII; Don Davis, American Friends Service Committee (AFSC) Archives, who steered me to the Swarthmore Peace Collection and allowed me access to the AFSC Archives as well; Emily Sekine who helped me gather information about Kiyoshi and his family; and Marvin Weisbord, author of *Some Form of Peace*, who also suggested contact ideas for this book, leading me to more information.

This work was many years in the making and I thank my daughter Jenna Harris and her husband Ben Harris who inspired me all along with way; Hayes Alexander III who provided thoughtful feedback of my various drafts; Cousins Geoff and Peter Stich who shared their own insights about my father and our shared childhood memories; Ramona Holmes who inspired me with her memoir of her father; Michelle McDowell and her creative genius who designed the cover; all the friends and family who continued to encourage me over the years, too many to mention; talented creative nonfiction writing instructors Jonathan

Callard, Kase Johnstun, Lise Funderberg, Annie Nguyen, and the students in the creative writing classes who provided encouragement and feedback along the way.

About the Author

D R. DEBORAH RANNIGER retired in 2018 with over twenty-five years of leadership experience focusing on nonprofit management and government. She served as the Executive Director of Etta Projects, an international nonprofit, as well as the ED of two community college foundations. As an elected official for the Kent, WA, City Council, she was instrumental in integrating equity and inclusion in the city's strategic plan, helped to spearhead the replacement of the ailing community pool, and fostered many enhancements to the Park and Human Services system during her twelve-year tenure and chair of that committee. She is a practicing visual artist, grant writer, urban chicken egg farmer and occasional foster dog mom. She attended Cal Arts and the University of Washington graduating with undergraduate degrees in Art, Landscape Architecture and an MA and PhD in Speech Communication, all of which she enjoys using to help make the world a better place.

www. hellgatepress.com

Made in the USA
Middletown, DE
29 August 2022

72595031R00080